LAWRENCE
of Australia

PERSIST.

Laurie Lawrence

**IRONBARK
PRESS**

LAWRENCE of Australia

STORIES OF INSPIRATION

told by
LAURIE LAWRENCE

IRONBARK PRESS

Dedication

Citius, Altius, Fortius
This book is dedicated to every young athlete
who dares dream the Olympic dream of
faster ... higher ... stronger.

Published in 1993 by Ironbark Press
Level 1, 175 Alison Road, Randwick NSW 2031

National Library of Australia
Cataloguing-in-Publication

      Lawrence, Laurie, 1941-
      Lawrence of Australia

     ISBN 1 875471 24 3

     1. Athletes - Australia - Anecdotes.
     2. Olympics - Anecdotes. I. Title.

    796.092

Editor: Ian Heads
Production: Ian Heads and Geoff Armstrong
Design and Finished Art: Hugonnet Bouda Graphic Design
Cartoons and Cover Design: Scott Rigney
Front cover photography: Ern McQuillan
Printed by Southwood Press, Marrickville NSW

Photographs: The photos for *Lawrence of Australia* were gathered from a
number of sources. Special thanks to the AAP Photo Library for the
photos on pages 90, 217 and 261, and to the people at the News Limited
photo library, and photo sales, for the News Limited shots used in the
book. The publishers would also like to thank the following photographers whose work appears: Craig Borrow, Colin Bull, Jim Fenwick,
Graeme Fletcher, Roy Haberkamp, John Hawlyruk, Peter Kurnik, Warwick
Lawson, Ern McQuillan, Terry Phelan, Barrie Ward and Leigh Winburn.

Back cover photo: Laurie Lawrence, immediately after Duncan
Armstrong's win in the 200 metres men's freestyle final at the
1988 Seoul Olympics.

Contents

Preface   6
Introduction   9
Foreword, by Phil King and Debbie Flintoff-King   13

Section 1: Some Morals

1 The Beginning ~ Helen Gray   17
2 Never Judge a Book by its Cover   29
3 Positive Power ~ Tracey Wickham   39
4 One Step at a Time ~ Glenn Buchanan   53
5 Belief ~ Jules   67
6 Building a Team ~ The Fishing Trip   79
7 Realisation of Dreams ~ Edwin Moses   91
8 Steep Roads Lead to High Mountains ~ Jon Sieben   97
9 Power of the Pin ~ Dawn Fraser   111
10 Drastic Steps ~ Julie McDonald   121
11 Champions Come in all Shapes and Sizes
   ~ David Berkoff   137
12 A True Champion ~ Debbie Flintoff-King   145
13 Doing What the Opposition Won't
   ~ Duncan Armstrong   155
14 Master Planner ~ Phil King   169

Section 2: Some Memories

15 Midnight Madness   177
16 The Gold Medal Bar   185
17 You Need Friends   193
18 Stanley ... Steve Holland   201
19 Seoul '88 ~ Reflections on a United Team   211
20 Barcelona Memories   217
21 Being Professional ~ Lisa Curry-Kenny   227
22 Olympic Apologies to Banjo   233
23 Galloping Gold   245
24 Born to Win ~ Kathy Watt   255

Preface

Laurie Lawrence's achievements as a supreme mentor of young Australian sporting champions sometimes get lost in the version of him that television has imprinted on the nation's consciousness. The images of a burst of manic behaviour at poolside during a major meet, or of Laurie bashing his (bronze medal) charge Glenn Buchanan over the head with a rolled-up programme at the 1984 Los Angeles Olympics - before a vast TV audience - are hard to shake. The story he tells against himself in this book of a Melbourne petrol station attendant who recognised him, and declared: "Say, I know you. You're that swimming coach fellow from Queensland ... the silly one," will be met with a grin and a knowing nod from some.

There is far more of course to Laurie Lawrence than this emotional overflow which now and then sweeps him up in some eccentric deed. His growing-up years spent alongside a swimming pool in Townsville, he veered for a time into rugby union, achieving the singular honour of playing for his country, on the Wallaby tour of New Zealand in 1964. Battling asthma, he gave football away in the mid '60s and headed back to the warmth of Townsville where he began a career in swim coaching which was to bring astonishing success.

In the 1970s and '80s he was the inspiring motivational force behind a succession of magnificent achievers in swimming ... Stephen Holland, Tracey Wickham, Jon Sieben, Duncan Armstrong, Julie McDonald, and many more. Freestyler Armstrong, who forged a steely bond with Lawrence and went on to win the 200 metres gold at the Seoul Olympics of 1988, said of his coach : "He had that gift of inspiration. He could reach into you, and you could feel the strength from him."

Lawrence's own iron-hard philosophy of success was honed early, as he fought his asthma, and then at one stage a severe bout of pneumonia, which left him with permanent scarring of the lining of his lungs. A stanza written for the record he released in 1990, *I Australia*, identifies that philosophy:

> *Be proud, persist, work hard, stand tall,*
> *Don't quit, don't bend, don't break, don't fall.*

As coach, motivator and entertainer he employs the "knuckles down the wall" approach, always reaching out for his own personal credo: "Striving for Excellence".

Those messages provide the foundation stone for the success of all his swimmers, and for his own striking and varied successes in his working life. Rising at 4.30am every morning to superintend activities at his famous swim school at the Palm Beach-Currumbin Pool, where he has joined forces with former Olympic champion and world record-holder Michael Wenden, he lives by the tenet: "Rest is for the dead."

This book represents another facet of the remarkable persona of Laurie Lawrence. He wrote it himself, snatching time at airports and on flights to jot down yarns that are often hilarious and very often inspirational - of his experiences with champions of sport at Olympic and Commonwealth Games.

These stories of Fraser and Wickham, Sieben, Edwin Moses, Kathy Watt and all the others now provide the basis of Laurie Lawrence's extraordinary new career, as a compelling and inspiring guest speaker, doing the rounds of corporate Australia.

The latest development in his life is right on line for Laurie Lawrence ... with this Master Coach of swimming you get to expect the unexpected.

Introduction

My parents instilled in me a love of reading. Nowadays, because of my busy work schedule, my reading is mostly confined to a quick glance through the daily paper or a good short story. One day I was sitting relaxing, with a copy of Henry Lawson's *"The Loaded Dog"*, when it suddenly occurred to me that I'd like to write a book about some of the funny incidents that have taken place during a "flamboyant" coaching career that has spanned some twenty years. So I guess you'd say this book was inspired in some way by the father of the Australian short story.

I gave the matter serious consideration and finally decided to have a go. Many of the stories that appear in this book were written on planes. In my head there are more, half finished, waiting for a spark of genius. I've drawn on experiences which have taken me to three Commonwealth Games, three Olympic Games, World Swimming Championships and a host of international meets. At these events I've rubbed shoulders with and, in some instances, coached Commonwealth, World and Olympic champions - national treasures who have interesting, funny and heart-warming stories to tell. These "national treasures" were the people I wanted to bring into the living rooms and libraries of Australians.

With my teaching background, the aim was to do more than just tell a good yarn. I wanted, through these stories, to educate and influence the lives not only of the young swimmers with whom I associate, but also the lives of young and old people from all walks of life around the country. I wanted them

Facing page: Laurie Lawrence and Duncan Armstrong wearing gold medal grins, Edinburgh 1986.

to enjoy the stories, to laugh and cry with the characters, and experience the joys that come from dreaming ... and from chasing dreams.

Each story, then, is intended to be more than just a good yarn. Each has a moral. Each a modern-day sporting Aesop fable if you like! For example, the story which begins the book, on Helen Gray, who was my first Commonwealth Games and Olympic representative, is more than just a tale about a crazy young coach who, at his first major swimming competition, pelts a young girl's silver medal over the fence in disgust. The story endeavours to show how, in life or sport, it is important to analyse our current position and to re-focus our goals for the future. In this way we will continue to grow as individuals and experience the satisfaction that comes from dreaming, from setting goals and pursuing those goals.

The short story on Duncan Armstrong has its amusing side. However it is meant to dig below the surface and lay bare the extraordinary commitment of a young man striving for Olympic gold. It attempts to show that Olympic champions are prepared to pay the price, are prepared to focus on the task at hand. In this way they can proudly hang the Olympic gold medal around their necks - they have performed feats their opposition were not prepared to take on.

My story about Tracey Wickham attempts to show the character trait of determination which is inherent in world champions. In addition it expounds the values of self-esteem and positive reinforcement. It illustrates what can be accomplished if you try or, in Aussie lingo, "Have a Go!" There are many Australians out there now who have the latent ability to be great doctors, lawyers, carpenters, runners, swimmers, jumpers. Unfortunately these people have never been encouraged to "have a go" and so their talent withers on the vine. Perhaps this story will motivate the "Could Haves" to self-start and achieve.

The book is not meant to be a quick fix to get us achieving. It is meant to be a help, a guide, a companion in tough times.

Introduction

I wanted to show that dreams are important and we must hold onto those dreams. However without hard work those dreams are only fantasies. The perfect result is when we dream and then make those dreams come true. Only an individual with persistence and dedication can make a dream come true.

The choice is yours: if you want the edge in life or sport there are no shortcuts. You must work hard, make tough decisions, sacrifice, and march daily toward your goal one step at a time. If you are serious about winning, you must be prepared to win.

The will to win is the will to prepare to win,
The harder you work, the sweeter the victory.

Finally, in many stories the dialogue is a product of both memory *and* imagination. At times I have used poetic licence and, although the dialogue may not be word for word accurate, the meaning remains true. The story content throughout is based on real competitive experiences.

Section Two of the book has been entitled "Some Memories". These are more lighthearted. Read them and find your own moral. If not, enjoy the book! Tell your friends! If it helps one person expand their lives a little or achieve their dreams it will have served a purpose. If it doesn't do this, try at least to remember:

The harder you work, the harder it is to surrender.

Laurie Lawrence
March 1993

Foreword

One of the greatest thrills of our time in sport at the highest level is in the friendship that we have developed with Laurie Lawrence. The mere mention of the name "Lawrence" brings memories flooding back.

In 1984 Laurie Lawrence was "out of his tree" with joy as his young charge, 5ft 7in (170cm) Jon Sieben defied all the odds as he swam over the top of the albatross, 6ft 7in (200cm) Michael Gross, to win gold and set a world record in the 200 metres butterfly final at the Los Angeles Olympics.

Four years later Laurie "let the animal out", Duncan Armstrong, to achieve "the impossible" by defeating the greatest swimmer of the time, Matt Biondi. In doing so to the shout of: "Stuff the silver, we're goin' for gold!" Armstrong not only won the 200 metres freestyle gold medal at the Seoul Olympics - but, like Sieben, he also set a new world record.

It is defying the odds ... doing the impossible that excites Laurie Lawrence. He is the master motivator. He inspires confidence and belief. He also generates relaxation at critical moments. No challenge is too great; no task impossible. All around him soak up his enthusiasm.

To some people, Laurie Lawrence is a crazy, over-competitive madman - swimming's equivalent of Percy Cerutty. But what the public see is only one glimpse, one small side of the man. Apart from his will to win, Laurie Lawrence's greatest asset is his ability and attitude in helping young Australians achieve their goals. He feels deeply for every athlete in the green and gold - not just the ones he personally coaches. We

Facing page: A winning team - Debbie Flintoff-King and her husband and coach, Phil King.

have watched him lose six kilograms as he shared a weight reduction diet with one of his athletes - to help her win a Commonwealth gold. We've seen him cry for his athletes in hard times. We've witnessed him bring smiles to the faces of sick and injured athletes as he sang a song he had written especially for them.

It is the winning for Australia that counts with Laurie Lawrence. On swim teams he is inevitably regarded as the team's greatest asset because of this. It is through this philosophy, this approach that Laurie has been involved in many incidents and stories that over time will become Australian sporting folklore ... if they are not that already. The stories on these pages are not just about swimming.

Some of them will make you laugh, some will make you wonder and many will provide motivation and inspiration. We believe that all will provide great joy as you get the chance to share the unique experiences of one of Australia's greatest sporting personalities ... Laurie Lawrence.

Debbie Flintoff-King
Phil King
March 1993

Some Morals

Chapter I

The Beginning
~Helen Gray~

Nineteen hundred and seventy was a vintage year for Australian sports lovers. The armchair critics who spent their weekends perched in front of televisions sets, sipping on stubbies, cheering their favourite sportspeople and footy teams, had a fun time. Baghdad Note won the Melbourne Cup at 25 to one. I did my dough! John Newcombe beat Ken Rosewell in an all-Australian Wimbledon final. I backed Australia! Greg Chappell made his Test debut, and Australia reaped a harvest of 35 gold medals at the Commonwealth Games in Edinburgh. Carlton won the VFL Flag and Souths won the Sydney rugby league premiership.

Another stunning sporting achievement that year was not covered by any TV network. At the Queensland Swimming Championships, Laurie Lawrence - just four years into his coaching career - hurled Helen Gray's silver medal a hundred metres over the fence and onto the railway line at the starter's end of the Brisbane Valley Pool. The great Viv Richards would have had trouble getting the distance - in fact, the throw still stands as the record for the silver medal hurl at the Queensland Championships.

In 1970, I fancied myself as a smart young coach - come to think of it, still do. I flew down from the bush with a squad of superbly fit young swimmers, all starry-eyed, burnt brown from the hot North Queensland sun, aggressive and confident and all of them hunting gold medals. Being new in the coaching game, I was out to make a name for my Townsville team. My coaching philosophy had been moulded on the rugby field, an

Facing page: Aussie weightlifter Nev Perry hoists high 13-year-old Helen Gray, "baby" of the Commonwealth Games team in Edinburgh, 1970.

Lawrence of Australia

Laurie Lawrence, Queensland rugby star of the 1960s - in action in a Wallaby selection trial in 1964.

uncompromising win-at-all-cost attitude: "Winning was important ... why else do they keep the score?" For me, to come second was the pits. "Defeat", "failure", "can't" were words not found in my dictionary and were not to be tolerated in any of my young charges. Hell, it wasn't even worth the trip from the bush or the trouble of donning your Speedos to collect a silver or bronze medal!

Time and experience have made me revise and modify my attitudes slightly. Experience has taught me to race for gold uncompromisingly, ruthlessly, single-mindedly, competitively - to be tough ... but also to have a secondary goal: if you can't collect gold at least do your personal best time. Always be able to look back over your preparation and know you prepared to the best of your ability. Be honest, don't lie to yourself by looking for an easy option. There is none. This way you have

The Beginning ~ Helen Gray

the chance to always be a winner. You have to be able to look at yourself in the mirror every day knowing you've given it your best, knowing you have left no stone unturned in your quest for victory. Peace of mind and honesty with yourself are more important than all your records and gold medals. This simple systematic setting of realistic goals and the relentless pursuit of them keep the athlete involved in sport for many years and build a philosophy that can be used in life.

Remember: No-one ever drowned in sweat!

However, 1970 was early days in my coaching career and if you didn't have the gold medal in your hot little hand, then to me you were a loser, and all the effort had been in vain. I installed the "no guts no glory" attitude into the twelve young gladiators I had brought down from Townsville to make an assault on the Queensland Titles. We were here to win, not to have a good time.

After a magnificent race on the first night of the Championships one of my young warriors, Helen Gray, a strong, wiry, determined young girl with a flashing smile and short-cropped hair, who was later to represent Australia at the Commonwealth Games in Edinburgh and the Olympic Games in Munich, waltzed up to me with a silver medal. Helen sported a grin like a split watermelon.

This was a major blunder - smiling over a silver medal! I wanted her to go to the Commonwealth Games, and her smile, suggesting that sport was only for fun, was intimating that excellence and ambition could be compromised.

"Show me!" I spat. She pressed the medal into my hand and two point zero eight seconds later it was sailing over the Valley Pool fence with its barbed wire top. It landed on the Brisbane-Sandgate railway line at the starter's end of the Valley Pool. The Queensland record for silver medal hurl was established!

This impulsive action by a cocky young coach sparked immediate response from parents, coaches and officials.

"Who is that fool?" asked the referee.

Lawrence of Australia

MICHELANGELO'S
'LAURIE'
(THE MEDAL THROWER)

"Laurie Lawrence, former rugby player," whispered an overweight time-keeper to her bespectacled friend.

"We'll cite him!" snarled committee men.

"Suspend his coaching membership," snapped some older swim coaches.

"Best I see him in the QSA offices," offered Greg Lalor, chairman of the Association.

Helen was shocked. In her four years of racing this was the first time I'd reacted so strongly over a second place. Her lip quivered and she bravely fought back tears. Grandmothers, there to cheer on their little Dawn Frasers of the future, shook their heads and cried "shame! shame!" before popping another couple of glucose tablets into the open mouths of their young hopefuls, perched on the wooden stand like hungry young birds.

The Beginning ~ Helen Gray

Grim-faced officials went into huddles, planning disciplinary action, discussing ways to rid the sport of this new blight. Suzie Anderson, another of my budding champions who happened to get third in the same event and was prancing, smiling and happy just two steps behind Helen, witnessed the throw and froze in her tracks. The colour drained from her face as she quickly stuffed her precious bronze medal into her Speedo tracksuit top and zipped it up tight. It was safe there!

Alex Evans, an old rugby mate, bald head polished for the occasion, cheered, laughed, clapped - then abused me for not throwing it further. Alex was having more fun than on the day the Wallabies scored the pushover try against Wales on the Grand Slam tour of the British Isles. At Valley Baths that night the proverbial cat was well and truly amongst the pigeons. I'd committed an unpardonable offence. I'd pelted a hallowed Queensland medal over the fence, uttered numerous profanities as it sailed merrily on its way, and abused one of my young swimmers for losing. I had no shame, I had made a fool of myself. For sure it would be headlines in the next day's papers. It was my first state titles and here I was already in deep sh— with officials. What a way to start a career!

Later, Helen sat with me in a quiet section of the pool, her head bowed. "How do you expect to go to Scotland if you can't win a miserable Queensland title?" I quizzed her.

"I was tired from the eight kilometres you made me swim this morning," she snapped.

"Don't get dirty! I told you before the Championships we were not going to taper, you had to win untapered."

"Why didn't you kick into the wall?" I asked again.

"It's hard." A slight quiver in her voice.

"I don't care! So is making the Commonwealth Games team." "I'm so tired, Laurie, " she said. The quiver in her voice was stronger now.

"It's only a state of mind," I snapped. "You have to be contemptuous of pain. Welcome it as a sign of improvement and keep pressing against it."

Lawrence of Australia

"Laurie, I'm tired. Help me!". The tears welled in her eyes.

"Helen, things of value don't come by luck, they're won by pain and sacrifice! You must believe! How do you think Herb Elliott felt when Cerutty made him run the sand hills at Portsea?"

"I do believe Laurie ... I do," she answered. "But I'm so tired! Help me!" The tears rolled down her cheeks.

I weakened. "OK," I said, "I'll give you three days' rest. Light training - but I want a guts effort in the two hundred metres freestyle on Friday night. I want the gold!"

Later that night, by the light of the moon and a packet of Redhead matches, a smart-arse young swim coach with a Dennis Lillee moustache and well-groomed Elvis Presley side-burns was seen to rip his bell-bottomed trousers on the barbed wire as he scaled the Valley Pool fence, conspicuous in his ming-blue shirt and pointed-toe shoes as he began his search for a broken-hearted girl's discarded silver medal on the Brisbane-Sandgate train line.

The swimming fraternity, looking on, cheered loudly as the coach was almost run over by the 9.10 Sandgate Flyer. Two hours later, alone on the line, I cheered loudly myself when I found the medal wedged in a cracked railway sleeper.

I changed Helen Gray's training. I gave her three days of easy training, no sprints and booked her in for a massage by Bill Elvis, whom the young swimmers in Brisbane at that time saw as the Messiah of Massage. I bought her a new cap and goggles, and told her she was now ready to race the best in Queensland in the 200 metres freestyle championship - *no excuses!*

Helen won the gold medal easily in a new Queensland record time. She beamed proudly on the winner's dais as the medal was slipped around her neck, and waved to the North Queensland contingent who screamed their approval from the old wooden stands at the deep end of the pool. As soon as the medal presentation was over she marched back to the stands, stopped ten metres in front of me, and with all the audacity of youth, flung the gold medal at me with full force.

The Beginning ~ Helen Gray

"You wanted the gold medal - it's yours! Keep it!" she exclaimed. Quicker than any Australian slips fieldsman, my hand flashed upwards and I caught the shining medal as it sailed by my right ear. I slipped it into my trouser pocket.

To this day that medal has pride of place in my office as my most treasured piece of memorabilia. Eight weeks later, when announced as a member of the Commonwealth Games team for Edinburgh, 13-year-old Helen bounded up the stairs of the old North Sydney Pool looking for her coach. She was the youngest team member. "Yippee!" she yelled, and waved excitedly as she sighted me punching the air in ecstasy, high up in the stands. My first Australian representative! We met half way and hugged and jigged, we were savouring the moment of triumph, the moment when a dream is realised, a goal is achieved.

"It's over, I'm there, I've made it!" she whispered.

I stopped dead in the middle of our celebratory jig, my coaching instincts screaming: "Re-focus! Re-focus!" I stepped back, grabbed her by the shoulders, held her at arms' length, looked squarely into her eyes and said simply: "Helen, it's only the beginning."

She looked at me puzzled. "We must now work towards Edinburgh! You can be a medallist there."

"Do you think so?"

"I'm sure," I told her. So, a new goal was set.

I had to have her set a new, realistic, achievable goal or she would float through her swim career, drifting like thousands of poor unfortunate souls who wander through life, never achieving anything of note or value, never experiencing the hope of planning, not feel the joy of achieving, or the exhilaration of winning - because they don't have any specific, clearly identifiable objectives. Too many people have no dreams to chase, no rivers to swim, no mountains to climb.

My job now was to jolt Helen back to reality, to re-focus her thoughts, to develop a plan of action that would enable her to win a medal in Scotland. I had to have her understand and

Lawrence of Australia

Coach Laurie with Helen Gray, in Sydney in 1973.

identify the benefits of doing this, so that she would work to make that goal a reality.

"Helen you're in the team, and that gives you the opportunity to win a medal," I said.

"But Dad's happy with me making the team," she answered. "No buts - sure you're in the team, but that's all the more reason to try for a medal. You have a chance not available to the kids who didn't make the team. You've got to make your parents even happier by winning a medal."

"Do you think I can make it?" she asked.

"Of course. You have to grasp this opportunity in both hands and work towards winning a medal."

"I'm only thirteen."

The Beginning ~ Helen Gray

"Good! Gives you more chance. Edinburgh is six months away, you'll improve more than any of the older girls - just on growth alone."

"But Karen's the world record holder."

"Then you'll have to break the world record," I joked.

She laughed."I'd like to," she said.

"Can you imagine the town if you did?" I said. "They'd go berserk! Huge party! Parade through the city streets, unbelievable!"

"Do you think I could?" she asked again, her eyes lighting up.

"Break the world record?"

"No, silly!" she giggled. "Win a medal!"

"No risk - piece of cake! I can see you in Scotland, gold medal hanging around your neck, shining gold-coloured ribbon. I can hear the national anthem. You standing there so proud!"

"It's winter in Townsville, the water will be ice-cold for training, " she said. She was back to reality. Teenagers have a way of arguing.

"Helen, nothing of value ever comes easy. If you want something badly enough, you have to put up with some inconveniences along the way."

"You ever swim in cold water?" she queried.

"Not the point," I dismissed. "Cold water will be only a temporary inconvenience. A problem you have to thrust out of your mind."

"Yeah, but in winter it's cold and dark Laurie. I don't like cold and dark."

My mind raced. What could I say? "True, but we can change the training times and days, " I finally offered. "If we train on Saturdays and Sundays instead of having a day off we can train in the warmest part of the day. That will eliminate three early morning training sessions and you'll get a great tan! See, you will only have to swim in the dark two mornings a week, on Tuesday and Thursday ... easy!"

"What about Monday, Wednesday and Friday mornings?"

"Sleep in!"

"What! Going soft?"

"Well, if you really want to beat Karen (Moras), you could get up at 7am and do an hour of exercises before you go to school on those days."

"We could buy a set of Forbes Carlile rubbers and a Ryde T-shirt."

"Why?"

"You could put the T-shirt on the floor, pretend it's Karen's and try to drip sweat on it as you exercise."

"Laurie, you're crazy!"

"Yeah, wouldn't it be sensational to use Forbes' rubber pulleys and T-shirt to motivate you to beat his world record holder!"

"I'd like to try," she said.

"Me too," I answered. "See you Monday."

As she turned and walked away, I called: "Helen."

"Yes."

"I'm sorry I pelted your silver medal away. I was wrong."

"That's okay," she grinned. "I'll try for gold in Edinburgh."

In my heart I knew she was too young at thirteen to beat a world record holder, but by setting her goal of beating the great Karen Moras, I felt confident she could work towards being the youngest swimmer to win a medal in Edinburgh. Browning's words flashed into my mind:

A man's reach must exceed his grasp
Or what's a heaven for?

Helen went on to the Commonwealth Games in Edinburgh on her own and covered herself in glory, while I headed for America to link with Olympic coach Don Gambril's swimming team, hungry for more information on training programmes, butterfly techniques and medal throwing. In Edinburgh Helen Gray was the youngest girl to win a medal at the Commonwealth Games of 1970.

The Beginning ~ Helen Gray

Footnote:

Helen, now married, still swims for fun in the Aussie Masters' Competition. Occasionally we sit down over a cup of coffee and reminisce on the good old days. There is nothing so fleeting as a sporting event, but better still ... nothing so lasting as the memory of it.

I am now teaching Helen's 12-months-old son Nathan to swim. I hope he is a good boy and that I don't have to throw any of his toys over the fence.

Chapter 2

Never Judge a Book by its Cover
~Peter Evans, Neil Brooks~

You wouldn't find Peter Evans in a fancy gym pumping iron, glancing at developing biceps in giant floor-to-ceiling mirrors, flexing triceps, wearing hugging lycra cycle pants that accentuate certain sections of the anatomy, or oiling his body and brushing his hair back to catch the ladies' attention. You would have much more likely mistaken him for the puny weakling who had sand kicked in his face on the beach.

My first close contact with Peter Evans, a slender, sandy-haired West Australian with turned-out feet and a warped sense of humour, came at the Australian team headquarters, the Coogee migrant hostel in Sydney, while we were preparing for the 1982 Brisbane Commonwealth Games.

It was hard to believe that this man was Australia's most successful breaststroker of the 1980s, with a gold and a bronze medal from the 1980 Olympics in Moscow among his souvenirs. He would subsequently add to his collection a gold medal at the Brisbane Commonwealth games and two Olympic bronze medals in Los Angeles. Never judge a book by its cover. Peter Evans was a great racer, one of the best - a swimmer you could count on in a crisis.

In 1980 as he, Neil Brooks, Mark Tonelli and Mark Kerry were winning gold for us in the 4 x 100 metres medley relay at the Moscow Olympics, I was, along with millions of other patriotic Australians, glued to the television set, screaming my

Facing page: Big Neil Brooks (right, pictured with Mean Machine teammate Greg Fasala), who came to the rescue of Peter Evans in Brisbane in 1982 - in an incident which has become part of swimming folklore.

assistance to the quartet. We know they couldn't have won without our cheering. In fact at Olympic Games and Commonwealth Games times it is mandatory for anyone calling himself an Aussie to spend hours in front of the idiot box cheering for our sporting representatives.

Peter Evans amazed me. He certainly wasn't my cup of tea as a dedicated, hard-working, disciplined swimmer. Hell, I had eight-year-olds with better training habits! But he was a racer - and that's a key ingredient in any successful competitor. I was used to the work ethics of such swimmers as Steve Holland and Tracey Wickham who took pride at being first into the pool. So Peter's training philosophy came as a huge shock. At training he took pains to make sure he was last into the water ... and first out. He preferred sunbaking to training. Most swimmers do, but Peter actually practised what he preached. He would spend hours on the pool deck, walking, pointing, laughing, relaxing, while the other swimmers slogged the miles, practised their dives, worked on their turns. In fact, if you weren't familiar with the team composition you would have been forgiven for thinking Peter Evans was an extra-young coach, put on the team for experience. How did he perform so well? He was a racer, that's how - the ultimate competitor, with superb mental toughness.

One of the real characters of the 1982 Brisbane Commonwealth Games, Peter (motor mouth) was never lost for words, nor short of practical jokes. He helped maintain sanity in the team when we were housed at the "Coogee Hilton" in preparation for the battles ahead in Brisbane. He was first man to every party and last to leave. If there wasn't a party on, he was organising one. He loved life, and lived it to the full. His cup ran over.

Evans and big Neil Brooks were West Australian soul mates - the odd couple - Danny De Vito and Arnold Schwarzenegger, inseparable, bonded together by the magnificent Olympic relay gold medal in Moscow. Peter Evans' main competition in Brisbane was his complete antithesis, Victor

Davis, the world record holder. Davis, as the Americans might put it, was "one mean son of a b——"... an animal. Victor got as much fun out of terrorising his opponents out of the water as he did from beating them in the pool. He was the type of person kindergarten teachers handcuff at lunchtime. He would come out to race more like Muhammad Ali, the heavyweight boxing champion, than a swimmer.

Such was his lasting presence and impression on me, I need only to close my eyes to visualise him shadow sparring, dancing onto the Chandler Pool deck in his white Canadian knee-length robe with red maple leaf on the back, hood pulled over his head, snorting fire - waiting for the bell to ring. Removal of the robe revealed a magnificent physical specimen: suntanned, stomach rippling, muscle toned, hair curly and bleached, teeth even and pearly white. He was an awesome sight, and the vision of him is a sporting image I'll treasure for life.

Modern sports psychologists impress upon athletic coaches the importance of mental domination of opponents. Somehow, somewhere, sometime before the race, you are told to seek out a chink in your opponent's mental armour and exploit any mental weakness he may have. Exude confidence. Victor Davis was a master at it.

His pre-race ritual was enough to intimidate even the most experienced competitors. He would shadow box, bound, skip, stalk the pool deck - commanding the attention of spectator and competitor alike, before lying on the deck beside the racing block and plunging his magnificent, well-oiled body into the beckoning water. Any opponent not accustomed or alert to this domination ritual - although physically harmless, like the chest-beating of the mountain gorilla - was often beaten before the starter's gun sounded, psyched out and intimidated by Victor's very presence.

On the morning of the heats of the men's 100 metres breaststroke in Brisbane the awesome sight of Victor Davis greeted Peter Evans. Peter was by then a seasoned competitor, steeled to not be intimidated by such a peacock display. He was, however, slightly nervous; all good competitors get nasty butterflies immediately before they compete. Nevertheless, Evans was determined to race tough, and do his country proud. No one in their wildest dreams could predict what was about to happen.

"Take your mark!" There was a slight movement from the swimmer on lane six. "Stand up gentlemen. Please!"

Too late. The swimmers, bodies coiled, ears tuned, straining - listening for the slightest sound and poised for instant reaction - false started. Victor Davis, the ultimate competitor, used the false start for his maximum advantage, making a split second decision to further intimidate his Australian opponent. As he hit the water he immediately changed direction. Swift as an ocean predator, he swirled under the lane rope, brushing against a relaxed Peter Evans. Peter was not expecting the stray foot or wandering hand which ripped his goggles off. Thousands of skin divers throughout the world will attest that the sensation experienced when the clear vision afforded by a good pair of goggles becomes suddenly blurred is highly disconcerting. When the sensation is accompanied by swirling water and body contact with a huge predator, it becomes bloody frightening.

Peter emerged from the pool clearly upset - bewildered and unnerved. Nearby, Victor Davis snarled and prowled the deck, a wild animal in complete control.

"Behind the blocks, gentlemen!" "Take your mark!"

BANG!

Davis was ready. A magnificent dive with perfect stream-lining saw him spear to the lead. A beautifully controlled first 50 metres, a well executed turn, and a powerful finish saw Victor make the heat a one-boat race. Davis controlled all, the pool, his opponents, the deck for a magnificent heat win - and a huge psychological advantage over all opposition.

Victor Davis - Round One.

"Honestly Brooksie, he kicked me," wailed Peter Evans,

brushing his hair vigorously as he dried it.

"What?" questioned the big man incredulously.

"He kicked me!"

"How?"

"When we false started, going back to the side his foot kicked my face."

"You sure?"

"Yes!"

"It must have been an accident. This is swimming, not kick boxing."

"Brooksie, he did it on purpose. He laughed at me afterwards. It scared me!"

"The bastard ! Wait till tonight!" snapped Neil Brooks.

"All I want is a fair go Brooksie," responded Evans.

"Tonight you shall have it," said the affable two-metre giant. "Leave it to me. You worry only about your race."

The great Canadian breaststroker Victor Davis.

That night I drove a happy Australian team to Chandler in my old Bedford bus. The spirits were high, all the windows were open, and strains of "Waltzing Matilda" greeted spectators and families who thronged to the pool to hunt autographs and watch their Australian heroes battle the Canadians, the Poms and the other Commonwealth cousins. Brooksie sat at the front of the bus. Pensive. Staring out the window, deep in thought. I stopped the bus close to the entrance and he was first out. He strode purposefully towards the pool, brushing through the swelling crowd, oblivious to the back-slapping and well wishes of the crowd.

"Good on you Brooksie," one fan yelled. "Love your bald head!" from another."What are you doing tonight Neil?" cooed a sweet 16-year-old. "The Mean Machine's great!" cried a young boy with close-cropped hair.

"Yeah! The Mean Machine's great!" chorused his three mates. They too had close-cropped hair. "Yeah! but you're the best Brooksie," yelled the one with the shortest hair.

All the remarks fell on deaf ears. Neil Brooks didn't even notice the little autograph seekers with whom he would normally stop and joke for twenty minutes as he signed. His mind was totally pre-occupied. Victor Davis' curly hair and flashing smile neoned into his subconscious. He hurried into the pool. He couldn't wait.

The pool was brilliantly lit. Team banners from all countries covered the chairs. Uniformed officials busies themselves arranging timing gear, tightening backstroke flags, checking false start ropes, wheeling in the electronic touch pads. The announcer put on the "Men at Work" song used by our victorious America's Cup yachtsmen: "I Come From A Land DownUnder", and it blared from the loudspeakers. Spectators started to fill the stands. The well-informed ones were there to watch the warming up; the racing atmosphere at Chandler was slowly building to a crescendo.

Brooks missed it all. He threw his green and gold team swimming bag onto the red plastic chairs reserved for the Australian team, sprawled himself over a chair, and waited, waited and watched. He was more like a wild animal stalking prey than an athlete waiting to compete for his country. Once he stood up and paced the deck, eyes squinting, never leaving the entrance. Alert!

The English team arrived, the Kiwis next. Finally the Canadians filed through the door, laughing, skylarking, twirling towels. Victor Davis was the centre of attention. Eyes shining, sunbleached curls, perfect teeth. Brooksie spotted him and stiffened. His eyes narrowed even further. He had found what he was waiting for - his prey had arrived. The next three quarters of an hour must have been an eternity for him as he stalked Victor Davis, waiting for an opportunity to pounce. His eyes never left the Canadian hero. Like the jungle cat he was patient.

Victor was relaxed and confident. Smiling, he went through his normal pre-race stretching warm-up slowly and deliberately. This complete, he loosened up in the water with some easy swimming, and kick and stroke drills, before signalling his bald-headed, gravel-voiced coach, Cliff Barry, to time his pace work and check the small specifics in his dives and turns.

Finally, Victor was ready! He eased his magnificent body out of the water and headed for the dressing rooms to change into his racing suit. Brooksie watched. Stiffened. Stood upright, and seized his opportunity.

He followed silently, two paces behind, seeking the privacy of the dressing room to confront Victor ...

The rest is Canadian or Australian folklore, with variations depending on who is telling the story. This is how I'm told the confrontation went:

"Victor!"

"Yes man?"

"Victor!" Brooksie raised his voice and spun Victor around to face him. Brooksie towered above him. "I just want to warn you about Peter Evans, Victor!" Brooksie hissed. "If you so much as touch a hair on his head tonight, I'll personally put my fist down your throat, and pull your arse out of your mouth!" With that the leader of the Mean Machine, bald head glowing, spun on his heel, and marched onto the pool deck to rejoin his Aussie team-mates - his mission accomplished, relieved and confident that his little mate Peter Evans would now have an even chance. The race for the gold would come down to physical ability not physical intimidation.

Canadian folklore has the same story up until the dressing room interlude - then the interpretation strays: "Victor, about Peter Evans ..."

"Piss off Neil!" snapped Davis. "Let the little jerk look after himself, I'm too busy preparing for a gold medal performance to be worried by your whingeing." With that Victor spun on his heel and stormed out of the dressing shed leaving big Brooksie stunned and stammering for words.

I'm not sure which version you prefer or believe. Whatever happened it made no difference to the results in the breast-stroke final. Victor Davis was too fast, too aggressive, just too good. He was *lord* of the breaststroke at the Commonwealth Games in Brisbane with two gold medals. He was the king.

Peter Evans won gold too in Brisbane - as a member of the

Never Judge a Book by its Cover

4 x 100 gold medley relay team. But in the breaststroke finals he had to be satisfied with minor placings behind a great champion - the awesome Victor Davis.

Footnote:

In 1989, the swimming world was stunned to receive the news that Victor Davis was dead. He had seemed invincible. "How could this happen?" we wondered. He had been the victim of a speeding car. The details are obscure and sketchy. Victor, in the company of a young lady friend, had argued with some young men at a Canadian night club. The young men left. Victor pursued them outside, and in an attempt to stop them, stood unflinching in front of their fast-approaching car. Victor was no match for the car, and the attribute that made him world champion - his fearlessness - undoubtedly contributed to his death.

God bless Victor Davis. He left the world with many great sporting memories and I reckon he'd still be up there fighting in Heaven ... I just hope Saint Peter doesn't want to race him.

Chapter 3

Positive Power
~Tracey Wickham~

In 1981 Tracey Wickham was on a comeback trail. Three years earlier, as an exciting 15-year-old freestyler, she had had the swimming world at her feet. In 1978 she was champion of the world. In 1980, two years older and stronger, she was expected to go to the Olympic Games in Moscow, line up as a mere formality and collect her gold medal. Unfortunately, because of international diplomatic problems associated with Soviet troops invading Afghanistan, politics reared its ugly head into sport once more. America boycotted, and called for support. Well-intentioned politicians interfered, and tried to dictate that the Australian team should also boycott Moscow. The Australian Olympic Committee stood firm, declaring that the Olympic ideals would be supported. When negotiations failed with the AOC the Government changed tack and brought pressure on individual athletes and coaches to boycott. Some of them did.

In my experience, athletes - be they East German, Chinese, Russian, African or English - are not interested in petty politics. They are not interested in the fighting or political bickering in which they so often become the pawns. The major consideration among all true athletes is competition. It doesn't matter where you come from, what religion you practise, or what colour your skin is, good healthy competition breeds friendships in the athletic arena - friendships that can last a lifetime.

Tracey, as an elite Australian athlete was caught up in the midst of the 1980 controversy. She was 17 then, and confused

Facing page: Tracey Wickham - a brilliant photographic study of the determination and concentration that helped make her a champion.

- and ultimately she decided not to compete in Moscow. By doing so she forfeited a chance to win an Olympic gold medal, and I'm sure she regrets her decision to this day. Among all the confusion and disappointment she announced her retirement. The disappointment was intensified when Michelle Ford, Tracey's greatest rival throughout her career, went on to be one of Australia's heroines. Michelle won Olympic gold in Tracey's world record event, the 800 metres freestyle, and so etched her name into Olympic history.

The combination of these events provided me with one of my greatest challenges: to make Tracey Wickham, world record breaker, really believe in herself once more and believe that she could once again be the best.

The first thing I did was to set out to make her feel good about herself, and good about her swimming. I can still remember the first day she came to Chandler Pool. I was on the coaching comeback trail myself and my squad consisted mainly of a crowd of little starry-eyed hopefuls. Tracksuited, she walked slowly into the dimly lit pool, with her favourite swimming bag (the one she'd used when she broke her first world record) slung loosely over her broad shoulders.

"She still looks trim and fit," I thought as she quickened her step towards me.

She waved, smiled and quizzed me in the form of a statement. "Laurie, I need a good swimming coach."

"Tracey, I need a good swimmer," I replied. And so the deal was done. Simply, quickly, efficiently. "Jump into lane zero and loosen up with an easy fifteen hundred," I called over my shoulder as I went to attend to my young hopefuls and to clear lane zero for her.

After stretching for fifteen minutes she took off her favourite Australian tracksuit, donned her cap and goggles, dipped her big toe into the pool to test the temperature, and dived in (it seems to be an unwritten law among competitive swimmers to test pool water with a big toe before diving in). She was on her way!

Positive Power - Tracey Wickham

I wasted no time! I grabbed half a dozen of my starry eyed hopefuls out of the pool. "That's Tracey Wickham, she's the world record holder," I told them. Look how well she is swimming."

"Oooh!" they chorused.

"Watch her streamline."

"Oooh!" they squealed in delight.

"Watch her tumble."

"Oooh!" They repeated.

It had become a fun game. The kids were loving every minute of it. And so was Tracey. "You walk up and down and watch her," I directed. And so Tracey became the Pied Piper of Chandler. Sometimes I would send them relay fashion. One little girl would walk four laps, the next little boy would walk four - eyes glued on Tracey. If she was doing a series of repeat 100-metre swims, then they would walk the relay with her again. I never let Tracey swim a lap that someone wasn't watching, walking, encouraging. They would walk while Tracey swam. Suddenly, Tracey, who had taken knocks and disappointments enough, for the first time in years started to feel really good about herself again. She started to look forward to training.

I kept up a barrage of positive reinforcements: "You look great ... you haven't lost it ... you're still the world record holder." Unbeknown to Tracey, I had these kids bring in autograph books and friends. These little ones didn't realise what an important part they were playing in Tracey's comeback.

Finally, it came. Dreaded January! Race time - the Queensland Swimming Championships, an occasion for the appraisal of form of all swimmers. It was to be Tracey's first official swim since her retirement after the Moscow fiasco. She was fairly apprehensive, genuinely unsure of her ability to swim fast again. She had only been back to training for a short while and she wasn't as fit as she would like to have been. The Australian Championships, fast approaching, were our major goal. We sat down and talked about her training programme, about what was best for her. After much consultation, we decided that the Queensland Championships were of secondary importance in the overall plan of getting her back into top shape, getting her back to swimming at her best.

"It's decided then," I said. "You're just starting to get into a bit of shape. If you don't race the Queensland Championships but train both morning and night while the Championships are in progress it will be better value for you in the long term." The plan was pretty well cut and dried. At that stage in her career, she needed to rebuild her self-confidence, self-reliance and self-esteem. In Tracey's mind the fact that she held every world freestyle record from 400 metres through to 1500 counted for naught. She wasn't afraid of work. (She just needed the occasional gentle nudge.) Her commitment to her work was excellent, in fact, a shining example for any young swimmer today.

We are all in control of our destiny but we need goals and direction. Unobtrusively at that time I was trying to focus Tracey's goals and direction. I was trying to introduce challenges so she could crystallise just where she was going. I'm sure this is what teachers, coaches, leaders and managers must do in life - have goals in place for our young charges to chase. If we set goals intelligently, and encourage young people to chase these dreams, they will achieve things they never believed possible. Our greatest natural resources are our children; they are there waiting ... untapped ... awaiting direction. They are the future of this great country of ours. We owe it to them to help them.

Tracey now had a goal. She wasn't going to race the Queensland Championships, she was going to train ... and train she did. The Queensland Championships are usually conducted over about eight days. Because Tracey, the world record holder, wasn't swimming, the press hounded her daily for a story. Was she going to swim in this event or that event? In fact, Tracey was generating more publicity than many of the girls who were racing in the Championships. It's a funny thing about life, that once someone starts to get a little bit more publicity than others in the same field jealousy can come creeping in. It appeared at that time that a certain amount of jealousy did start to surface as Tracey dominated local headlines. Some of the girls became openly antagonistic towards her.

It was now getting towards the end of the meet, a Saturday morning with only two days of racing left. Greg Lalor, the chairman of the Queensland Swimming Association, pulled me aside before the heats that day and said: "Laurie, for Tracey to get selected in the Queensland team to go to the National Championships, she must swim in this meet."

"Why?" I asked.

"It's not possible to select her, pay for her air fares and accommodation as part of the Queensland team unless she has actually swum in the meet," he answered.

"You fair dinkum?"

"The selectors have seen me and said it is not on."

"Thanks Greg."

"They want to check her race fitness."

"Thanks Greg, I understand!"

This exchange made me re-think my strategy. I had believed that Tracey being the world record holder, she would automatically be included in the team. I could see now that there would be a problem if she didn't swim.

This was Australia, not Europe. I went back to Tracey to explain the situation. She was in the 25-metre pool at Chandler, warming up for a training swim. I caught her eye and yelled:

"You flush with cash?"

"What?"

"You got plenty of cash?"

"Why?"

"Well, unless you swim one race to prove your fitness, you will have to go to the Nationals self-nominated, and pay your own way!"

"What?" she screamed incredulously. "They're a pack of B's. They know I'm training."

"Steady on Trace. Let's look at it sensibly."

"Sensibly? The bloody council are no help. They have me scraping five and ten cent pieces off the floor of the car to pay admission into this rotten joint and now the Swimming Association don't want me in the bloody team."

"No! No! They want you in! But you must prove your fitness. That's fair!"

"Oh bull!" she screamed, and stomped off into the women's dressing shed.

A wave of compassion came over me as she disappeared. I was having trouble coming to grips with the way we Australians treat our sports stars. I thought about Australia's only current world record holder, the woman to whom the local council gave a civic reception; the woman who started the ticker tape street cavalcade tradition in Brisbane when she returned home a heroine, victorious from the Commonwealth Games and World Championships in 1978. I thought about the four magnificent swims in which she broke three world records, won double gold at the Commonwealth Games in Montreal and double gold at the World Championships in Berlin. I thought about the enjoyment, the pride, the dreams, the pleasure she gave millions of Australians. I thought about councillors, politicians, dignitaries lining up for photographic sessions with her - yet they couldn't afford a gold pass to let her into the pool! To this day our world champions still have to pay to get into the pool.

I boiled, but it made no difference. Tracey had to swim to get selected. She came from the dressing sheds and I cornered her.

"Trace, you only have to race the 100 metres freestyle." I said.

"But I'm not a 100-metre swimmer," she countered.

"I know, but Mr. Lalor has told me all you have to do is swim the Queensland Championships if you want to be selected to go to the Nationals."

"They know I can swim. I'm the world record holder!" she spat back.

"Tracey, the selectors cannot select you unless you swim. This is Australia, not Europe. Now I'm not saying that you have to go out there and break a world record. Hell, it's only 100 metres, and you know that you don't even get warmed up over that distance."

"But all those sheilas will ... "

"Tracey, I'm not worried about what they think, or do, or what anyone else thinks or does for that matter. All I'm saying is: can you afford to pay your own air fares and accommodation to the National Championships?"

"You know I can't."

"Well Trace, it's a dash for cash."

She gave a half laugh.

"All you have to do is swim to get selected and have your way paid, otherwise we are in trouble financially."

"Let me think," she mused. She spun on her heel and disappeared. I didn't see her for half an hour.

Then she was back. "OK, I'll swim, " she said. When have I got to race?" she said.

"Well, the heats are on in an hour, so have a loosen up. Do a couple of short sprints to get the feel of going fast, because you haven't done any speed work at all."

"OK, just as long as you don't expect too much," she said impatiently.

"Tracey, I don't expect too much. I told you right at the beginning of the Championships that these weren't important, that we were really aiming at the Nationals. "OK! OK! Don't lecture me!"

Slowly that morning Tracey came around to thinking that she was going to go alright. Word travelled on the swimming grapevine very quickly that Tracey Wickham was going to swim in the 100 metres freestyle. All the young kids around the pool were rapt, and especially the young kids from our club who had been walking up and down with her during her lonely training sessions.

They called the women for the 100 freestyle heats. At the assembly point were a couple of Australian representatives who Tracey had often raced. Rivalry is a part of racing, and sometimes the rivalry has a special edge. When Tracey walked into the marshalling area. Lisa Curry was there with a couple of her friends, smiling and talking. They looked up at Tracey, mildly stunned. Lisa was fast, more of a sprinter than Tracey.

Tracey came in cautiously, like a wounded animal. Suddenly, whether in jealousy, or in jest, the girls waiting in the marshalling area slow-handclapped her. It was like waving a red rag at a bull. The hairs bristled on the back of her neck and she stalked the marshalling area, not speaking to anyone, not even Greta, the jovial marshal who fusses over all the swimmers like a mother hen. She stood in the corner, staring at the other girls. From Tracey there was silence, total defiance. She was like a caged wild animal, waiting to be released.

Her name was called. She growled and lined up. She swam her heat, qualifying safely for the final, then sprung out of the pool, and strode back to tell me what had happened in the marshalling area.

"Are you sure?" I asked.

"I'm, I'm, I'm *bloody* sure!" she stammered in reply.

"Tracey, I think you're imaginin' it!"

"I know what happened!" she said.

"Tracey, I think you're going overboard."

"I know what happened! And tonight I'm going to have my revenge. Now I'm going home to sharpen my claws."

There is nothing in sport quite like a world champion with bristles up. World champs don't need any motivating! Ever since the other girls had supposedly slow-handclapped Tracey, she was now desperate to beat them in their favourite event. Tracey Wickham was never a sprinter. I don't think there was ever an occasion where she made the Australian 4 x 100 metres relay team. Some of the girls involved in the incident that morning *were* members of the Australian sprint relay team.

Most times people respond best to positive motivation - but sometimes a simple taunt from an opponent can be enough to sting a champion into action.

Tracey went straight home and had a bite to eat. She chose her lunch very carefully for maximum nutritional benefit. She ate slowly and deliberately, and then went to bed. She lay there all afternoon, resting, and thinking about the job at hand, and what she had to do that night. In the evening I got to the pool early. Tracey was there before me. She had her mind set on one thing and one thing only. She was determined to make these girls suffer for what they had done. I couldn't stop smiling. Really, I couldn't believe that the other girls had actually played into my hands. If they hadn't given Tracey a reason to win, I'm sure she would have just gone into the event for a swim, just to be part of the event to qualify for the Queensland team. She really had no desire to win the Open 100 metres freestyle. The slow handclap had played into my hands as a swimming coach and I had to capitalise on it. I started to niggle, to throw a few little barbs at Tracey.

"Imagine those girls, fancy them slow-handclapping you! What did they do that for?"

"I don't know!" She snapped.

"Are you *sure* they slow-handclapped you?" I taunted.

"Course I am, I'm not bloody deaf, am I? I was in there, I was looking straight at them. It was me they were doing it to, I'm sure."

"Tracey, maybe they were listening to some music."

"Laurie, who do you think I am? I'm not stupid! As soon as I came into the room they started on me."

"You sure they weren't clapping to their Walkman?"

"Don't talk rot!"

"Well Trace, I suppose the only thing you can do now is to beat them. Let's work out a strategy how you can do it."

"I want to beat these girls," she said. "I want to make these girls suffer for clapping me. I want that title."

Lawrence of Australia

Laurie and Tracey (now Ciobo), with Tracey's daughter Hannah.

I said, "steady on Tracey".

"No, I want to make them feel it. Let's show them that I'm not the world champion for nothing."

I could see the fiery redhead slowly starting to boil. She was psyched to race this event as much as she had been in any of her world record swims. We worked out a strategy utilising Tracey's strength; she was strong in the second part of her races because she was endurance-orientated. We figured that if she could swim fast down the first fifty and be within contact of Lisa and the other girls at the 50-metre mark, then she had every chance of beating them coming home. Be there early! The tactic was simply to be there at the 50 metres, then see what would happen coming home. Tracey was determined.

I remember the race vividly. Take your mark, everyone up, ready, GO! Tracey left the blocks like a bullet. I had never seen her move so fast down the first fifty in all my life. She clawed over the top like a water spider. It was a great race, with the girls stroking down the first lap as one. Normally by the 25-metre mark, Tracey, because of her lack of speed, would be at least half a body length behind. In this race, for the first time in her life, she was only a head behind Lisa Curry at the 25-metre mark - and Lisa was obviously pushing it. Tracey's arms were flying. She was working a two-beat kick like she had never worked it before. They approached the turn - Tracey accelerated. I swear it was the best turn of her entire career. She didn't slow down at all going into the wall - she simply used it to change direction. She flipped fast, hit the wall and rebounded like a coiled spring.

Once the two girls hit the wall together, I felt that Tracey had every chance of winning the event. She used her old 400-metre distance turn, where she came up very shallow and sprinted out.

All the other girls used sprint turns, pushing deep in an attempt to get out under the rough water. But the rough water didn't worry Tracey. She buffeted and bullocked her way through it, and skipped along the top of it. She was heading for home, her tail up now - and the other girls just couldn't match the strength and ferocity she applied in that second fifty metres. She powered home, and touched the wall first, to an enormous roar from the crowd.

A Wickham victory salute - and the Queensland Women's 100 metres Freestyle Championship was hers. No one had given her a chance. Her time was a career best, and the crowd, the club, and all the young kids, their mothers and fathers in our club gave her a standing ovation.

It was a simply sensational performance from Tracey.

Now she was at her sickly best: she leaned across the ropes, offered her condolences to the other girls, shook hands, and smiled sweetly ... "What kept you darlings? Oh, I didn't think that I could possibly swim that fast. I can't *believe* I swam that fast. Do you think that they will put me in the relay team now? If they did put me in the relay team, would I be anchor girl? Lisa, what time do you have to do to be captain of the team? You know I've been sick!" ... And on and on she went.

Lawrence of Australia

Tracey Wickham came back magnificently to win double gold at the Brisbane Commonwealth Games of 1982.

Positive Power - Tracey Wickham

During the presentation, Tracey wore the biggest smile you have ever seen. The other girls were subdued as she kept bludgeoning them: "Thanks girls, you know I've been sick!"

Tracey graciously thanked Mr. Lalor for having her swim the 100 metres freestyle.

She was duly selected in the Queensland team to compete at the National Championships. Buoyed by her victory, she raced confidently to start a magnificent comeback which culminated with two gold medals at the Commonwealth Games in Brisbane. The highlight came after her win in the 400 metres freestyle when she was presented with the gold medal by the Queen.

Ask Tracey, though. I think you might find that she liked being Queensland Open 100 metres freestyle champion better than anything!

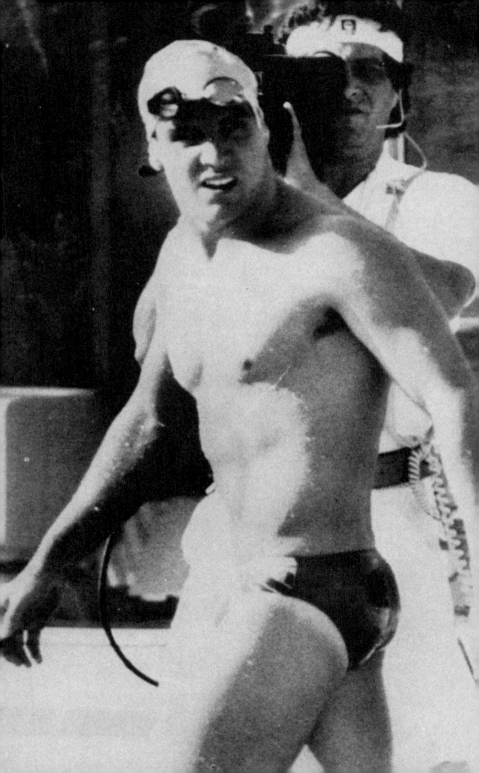

Chapter 4

One Step at a Time
~Glenn Buchanan~

The Australian team members cheered themselves hoarse on that eventful day in Los Angeles, 1984. Glenn Robert Buchanan jubilantly tossed the goggles he had borrowed from Shelly Pearson high in the air after his bronze medal performance in the final of the 100 metres butterfly. Michelle Pearson insisted that her goggles had brought him good luck. "You bloody beauty!" I screamed ecstatically, as I danced around and slapped head coach Terry Buck on the back, dislodging his glasses. I may have been a little over-vigorous.

Seventeen-stone Buck spun on me, adjusting his glasses, fire issuing through his nostrils.

"Fair go, Laurie!" he screamed. "That bloody hurt!"

"Sorry Terry!"

"You nearly broke my glasses."

"Sorry Terry!"

"Do it again and I'll rip your bloody arm off!"

"Sorry Terry!"

"You should know better! Get control of yourself!"

"Sorry Terry!" I was getting repetitious.

Then the big man softened, overcome by the emotion of the moment, and hugged me. We both did a little jig in the Australian section of the outdoor pool.

"If you get a gold you can belt me again! But only a gold! And Laurie ... "

"Next time wait till I take my glasses off!"

"Thanks Terry!" I screamed, and I started to take off. Terry's voice pulled me to an abrupt halt, as effective as a

Facing page: Glenn Buchanan checks the results-board after winning his heat of the 100 metres butterfly at the Los Angeles Olympics of 1984.

choker chain on a young Doberman.

"Laurie!"

"Yes Terry!" I stopped in my tracks, wanting to run, but respectfully obeying the head coach.

"Next time not so bloody hard, you hear! See ya!"

I took off like a scalded cat.

My excitement was at fever pitch, and had taken control of me. I had to see Glenn. I had to see the young man I'd taught to swim as a cheeky four-year-old.

"Be back soon ... I want to see Glenn!" I shouted, and jumped the security fence like a Grand National steeplechaser. I dodged American pool deck officials and security - who weren't nearly as zealous as their Korean counterparts would prove to be in Seoul four years later - and went looking for my young charge.

This was a moment very few coaches ever savour. For me it was a shining highlight of my coaching career. Many years before I had given Glenn Buchanan his first swimming lesson, and now I had guided him to Olympic success. I was stoked. My heart pumped as I searched for Glenn to congratulate him. I spied him being interviewed on national TV and hurtled towards him ...

"Well there it is Glenn, a bronze medal. You've achieved your wildest dream," declared Graham McNeice, live via satellite to Australia.

"Yeah, that's right Graham. It's something I've always dreamed about" said Glenn modestly, a smile lighting his face, his newly won bronze medal draped around his neck. Then he shook his head in disbelief and continued.

"I never thought it would come true. But dreams do come true if we work hard, and long enough."

"We were talking about it this morning," said McNeice, "two or three years ago you'd given up competitive swimming, then when the Commonwealth Games came along, you decided to have another crack, and you went back to your old coach Laurie Lawrence. He taught you to swim in Townsville?"

One Step at a Time - Glenn Buchanan

"Yeah, Laurie taught me to swim in Townsville when I was four." Glenn paused, "Yeah, he's an incredible guy!"

McNeice interrupted: "And speak of the devil, he's coming up behind you, now!"

It was at that point of the interview I arrived. With my rolled-up programme, I began belting Glenn about the head, whooping like a madman. Glenn covered up, and tried to protect himself with the flower arrangement which was given to all medallists. Graham McNeice, the true TV professional, put his arm around Glenn, and produced the understatement of the year:

"I think he's very happy! Don't you Glenn?"

"Yeah!" Glenn laughed. "I wish he wouldn't hit me though."

"What a sensational time? What? A second and a half faster?"

"Yeah! A second and a half faster than my best time!" said Glenn, looking over his shoulder, no doubt hoping that I would not persist with his public beating, on national television! McNeice continued: "I think he's very proud of you! Very, very proud!"

I'd let all my emotions bubble out naturally, and it was only later when I watched the television replay that I realised what I had done in the excitement of the moment. For me it was a special moment, captured forever on TV.

Glenn Buchanan's bronze medal in LA was the final chapter in a magnificent story about a remarkable man. Disillusioned after missing out on a Commonwealth Games team six years earlier, he'd quit swimming for the "Good Life", just as he was coming into his swimming prime. His swimming career unfulfilled, Glenn was inspired to make a return to competition, and have one last fling at international representation after watching Tracey Wickham's magnificent exploits at the 1982 Commonwealth Games in Brisbane. Glenn's bronze medal to me, was probably as satisfying as Jono Sieben's unexpected, unbelievable gold medal and world record swim in the 200 metres butterfly at those Games.

Sydney airport tomfoolery after the LA Games - only this time it's Glenn Buchanan (left) attacking coach Laurie.

I taught Glenn to swim, and moulded his career all the way up to that magnificent swim - a swim which was the absolute best he could do at that moment in his life. A coach can ask no more of his charge than that he or she achieve a personal best. That done, they can hold their head high, no matter what the outcome.

It all began when I was coaching Glenn's two older brothers at the beautiful Tobruk Pool on Townsville's palm-lined seafront. I was day-dreaming of Olympic Games, perfectly happy, when Les Buchanan, Glenn's dad, arrived accompanied by this little pocket dynamo. He had his beach towel slung over his shoulders, and was wearing green and gold Speedos, an old pair of goggles (borrowed from his brother) perched on his head. He was a real harum-scarum kid, the youngest of four boys raised on Dr. Spock.

"What can you do with this young fella?" Les inquired dryly.

One Step at a Time - Glenn Buchanan

"How old is he?" I quizzed.

"Four."

"Les, I don't start them 'til they're six!" I replied.

(This was in the years before I had any experience in teaching babies to swim.)

"Laurie, please! He's a big four," Les argued, while Glenn pushed the chest out, beamed, and fiddled with his goggles.

"Les, for safety reasons they have to be able to stand up in the big pool. I just can't take the risk!" I argued back.

"One of us - mother, grandmother or myself - will always be here with him. Try him! Try him!" he pleaded. "He's driving us crazy."

"Yeah, and you want him to drive *me* crazy!" I joked.

So, I took him. For his first lesson I put Glenn in the babies' pool and he cried for an hour and a half. Great start, I thought. Les sat quietly by, watching, waiting patiently, as I tried to control and reason with this squirming, kicking, crying four-year-old. Finally, we both called truce, and I let him run to his dad.

GLENN BUCHANAN RECEIVES HIS BRONZE MEDAL IN LOS ANGELES

"Good boy! You swim great!" enthused Les. "He went OK, Laurie. He went OK."

"What?" I asked, incredulously. I couldn't believe my ears. "He went good. Will you take him on? He's a strong four and I'm sure he'll learn to swim quickly. As you can see, he's got a bit of ginger in him."

I considered cutting my losses there and then, and sending him to terrorise Peter Tibbs. Peter, now a Cairns scuba diving instructor, was my rival swim coach in Townsville at the time. However, I'm a sucker for positive people, and Les was quietly persuasive, one of those characters who helps make Australia great and who are the backbone of many Australian families.

So, I resisted the temptation to axe Glenn's swimming lessons then and there. On reflection I'm sure life would have been a whole lot drearier had Glenn Robert Buchanan not stayed around.

I remember vividly the day I took Glenn into the big pool for the first time. It was a Tuesday morning in February, a day on which the tourist bus arrived at the Tobruk Pool to show inquisitive southerners where the great Dawn Fraser had trained, and broken many world records. Glenn's grandmother brought him down for his first swimming lesson in the big pool. "He's a strong boy at four," she enthused. She must have been under instruction from Les not to antagonise the coach.

By this time Glenn had mastered floating in the small pool, and was kicking at unbelievable speed for a small boy. His stumpy legs would thrash the water as he moved effortlessly from one side to the other of the little pool. I sat him on the edge of the Tobruk Pool with four other youngsters and slid into the pool, swimming out about five metres, ready to catch each child as they had their turn.

"How deep is it?" the wary little boy inquired.

"Just over your head." I replied.

"Will you catch me?" A tremor in his voice.

"Of course!"

"Where's grandma?" he asked uncertainly.

"She's watching."

One Step at a Time - Glenn Buchanan

"Where?"

"Over there," I replied, and pointed. That was my big mistake.

Once he knew where grandma was, he was off like a rocket, little legs pumping fast in her direction, with me in hot pursuit. "Grandma! Grandma! I'm sick!" he screamed, as he draped his dripping wet body around his grandma's legs.

"You'll be OK mate, grandma's here. Gee he's a strong boy Laurie," she enthused as I arrived, two steps behind, wondering how I'd let myself be talked into teaching this headstrong youngster.

But it was too late now. There was no turning back. I'd committed myself to Glenn's family and I had to complete the job, however distasteful. "He'll be right." I assured Glenn's gran, smiling through gritted teeth, and dragged him screaming and kicking back to the poolside.

"I'm sick! I'm sick gran!" Glenn pleaded, but to no avail.

Grandma was sympathetic, but firm, as grandmas usually are. "Back you go young man," she insisted.

Just as I sat young Glenn back on the poolside, the busload of southern tourists arrived. By now Glenn had decided that since he'd received no help from gran, he'd put some faith in his own legs. No way was he going to have a swimming lesson - and especially if he had to swim over deep water! He formulated a plan of attack. No sooner had I dived into the pool than Glenn was off again, stubby legs driving like pistons on an old steam train. He was at full speed, and no dumb old swim coach was going to catch him!

Well, he was quick for a four-year-old, but I'd played rugby for Australia, and was hot in pursuit. I brushed through the busload of tourists, who had gathered in the foyer, yelling an undignified "Excuse me!" as I chased the screaming child. Glenn headed out the front gate and off towards towards the beach, hollering at the top of his voice: "No! No! Save me! Save me! Grandma, save me!"

As I gave chase, one well-meaning old lady, sporting a

large white hat and coloured brolly, turned to her husband. "Did you see that Harry, a child molester? Follow him." "No, Maud." "Ring the police then, Harry!" "No, Maud." "There goes his grandmother. Help her!" "No, Maud, We'll mind our own business!"

Glenn was no match for my fast twitch fibres. I caught him and swooped him off his feet ten metres outside the front gate. The difficult part was bringing him back through the hostile tourists. Maud pushed forward brandishing her brolly. "You should be ashamed of yourself, young man!"

"Yes ma'am," I answered, and sidestepped quickly.

"Save me! Save me!" Glenn screamed, arms outstretched.

"You poor dear," Maud sympathised, then snapped at me: "Do you know what you're doing to this young child, you monster?"

"Yes, ma'am. I'm teaching him to swim." I sidestepped again and headed for the safety of the pool.

"Have you ever heard of the gentle method used by Forbes Carlile?" she screamed, and followed me towards the pool, waving her brolly threateningly.

"Yes, ma'am, I'm using that method right now," I called over my shoulder, as I jumped into the pool with Glenn draped, screaming around my neck.

"Well done Laurie," grandma smiled approvingly. And turning to Maud, with a dignity exclusive to grandmas said: "Madam, I would appreciate it if you would mind your own business." Maud left. Harry smiled.

Glenn survived his traumatic "baptism" and so did I. But from that day on I knew he was going to be trouble. As the years rolled by, Glenn developed into a real practical joker. As a ten-year-old during Townsville's rainy season, he would sit soaked to the skin, in a ten-inch puddle outside his home, smack bang in the middle of Mango Avenue. With only a pair of bike handle bars visible, legs outstretched and submerged, he would hold the handle bars in one hand and gesticulate with the other, redirecting traffic around the puddle.

One Step at a Time - Glenn Buchanan

Years passed. Glenn won Australian Age Championships, and, as did many other young swimmers, dreamed of representing his country. He tried for the Commonwealth Games in Edmonton, but missed, and like so many youngsters with broken dreams, he promptly retired. But in Glenn Buchanan, the dream of representing Australia was strong, and that dream was re-ignited four years later when he came to Brisbane to do a teacher training course at Kelvin Grove Teachers' College.

He watched Tracey Wickham's swims during the Commonwealth Games, and was inspired. He kept his dream secret from his parents, his sweetheart, and his coach for so long because of the insecurity, the improbability which surrounded it.

Then, in October 1982, he walked into the Chandler Pool. He still had his cheeky grin, but he was 30 pounds overweight. No one could have guessed his secret ambition - to become an Australian Olympian within two years!

"Hi Laurie! Room for a fat man?" he greeted me.

"Can you still swim?"

"Course! Not fast though!"

"What are you doing? What do you want?"

"Teaching course at Kelvin Grove. I'd like to get fit again," he said, patting his tummy. "Too much beer, too much good living."

"I don't mind you training here as long as you don't shirk training. I've got some pretty tough kids here, and I don't want them getting any bad habits."

"No problems! Where do you want me?"

"Lane two with all those young girls."

"What?" he said, but obeyed ... and soon found they were the toughest young kids he'd ever trained with.

The first six months of training were uneventful, humdrum and painful as he ground himself back into swimming fitness. He lost nearly fourteen pounds, survived my hell camp at Tallebudgera, and improved his 100 metres butterfly time from 68 to a sub-60 second swim in the Queensland Championships. It was nothing fancy by Australian standards, but he was starting to feel good and to get competitive. I talked to him about competing in the National Championships in Tasmania.

"Glenn, the club needs a couple of extra men for relays in Hobart for the Champion Club point score. Would you like to come?"

"Love to. Relays only?"

"Seeing you're going to do the relays, you may as well nominate for the 100 free and the 100 and 200 'fly for extra points."

"Not the 200 'fly. I'll never make it!"

"Do you want me to tell your little training mates, Jodie, Bronwyn, Peta, Raelene and the others that big tough Glenn chickened out, and let down the high standard of the 'Animal Lane?'"

"You wouldn't?"

"Wanna bet?"

"No! OK, I'll do it. I couldn't face those kids at training."

Four weeks later, straight and proud in his Queensland blazer, Glenn Buchanan stepped on the plane for Tasmania. The trip turned out to be mostly a fun time, but just before his race, he came up to me a bundle of nerves.

"Laurie, the butterflies are tearing my guts out," he said.

"Why?"

"I haven't raced for so long, I'm nervous. I'm packin' it!"

"Glenn," I replied, "Save your energy for the race."

"How?" he questioned.

"No matter how much you worry you won't be able to slow your opposition down, that's a fact. So why worry?"

"Yes, I know ... but ... "

"The only person you can control is you. Anxiety tenses, tightens and fatigues muscles, and burns energy. Lie down and focus on your swim, not the result. Plan and rehearse your race in advance. Listen to some music. Then, when you race, make the most of your opportunity. Racing is merely a celebration of talent. Just do your best."

One Step at a Time - Glenn Buchanan

He walked slowly away. I'd given him food for thought. In spite of his anxiety, he made the 100 metres butterfly final. One day after these National Championships Glenn collared me after training at Chandler Pool.

"Laurie!"

"Yes, Glenn?"

"Laurie, I ... "

"Yes, Glenn?"

"Laurie, I was wondering ... ah ... ah ..."

"Yes, Glenn?"

"I-was-wondering-if-you-would-coach-me-for-the-Olympics?" he blurted out. His dream was now public.

"Glenn, I don't know if you can make it, but we'll give it a bloody big shake, mate," I said - happy that he had now acknowledged and shared publicly his goal.

"Laurie, I don't want anyone to know. It's a secret dream. I don't know if I can do it, but if I don't at least try I'll regret it for the rest of my life."

"You've got nothin' to lose mate! Give it your best ... we'll all be proud."

"No one, not even Mary Rose (Glenn's girlfriend and now wife) must know," he said. "I want to do it on my own. Financially it's tough, but I want to give it a shot"

"Well, since you're serious, I have an old granny flat on my property in Miller's Road. If you help me paint it, make it presentable, you can stay there rent-free as long as you don't miss any training, and as long as you stay committed to your dream."

"You're on. When can I see it?"

"Tomorrow."

Next day, he and Mary Rose arrived for the inspection. The old disused granny flat underwent some hasty repairs. Every spare moment Glenn had over the next few weeks, he was there - painting walls and tiling the kitchen floor. Mary Rose worked just as hard - scrubbing, cleaning, hanging curtains, bringing in paintings and plants. Mal, his older brother, attended to the plumbing. The transformation was stunning. The trio turned the place into a presentable bachelor's flat, and it became the boys' home for the next eighteen months.

Once he had a permanent home, with reduced financial burden, Glenn was able to commit himself totally to his training. Each night, as an extra, he'd wander over and we'd do 500 sit-ups together on the lounge room floor. Things were progressing steadily. He was moving slowly towards his goal. One winter's morning around 4.15, when only the milkman, Kingston Town, T. J. Smith, crazy swim coaches and their equally crazy pupils are up, I called into "Frangipani Lodge" - the name we had given to the little flat. In good spirits, I arrived to wake up Glenn and the boys for the 20-minute drive to training. Michael Delaney, Mean Machine member, was staying with Glenn at the time.

Glenn decided he really didn't want to get up for training that morning. After all, the previous day there had been a going-away party for an old mate, a late night, a couple of pots and besides, it was bloody chilly! "Laurie, I'm going to skip training today," yawned Glenn. In such circumstances I'm not the most patient swimming coach in the world. However, I mustered my sweetest voice and said:

"OK, mate!" and went back to the main house looking for an ally. I found it in the shape of a blue plastic bucket.

I hope I am forgiven for what I then did ...

I raided the fridge and deep-freezer of all available ice cubes, and emptied them into the bucket. I made a fabulous cold-water poultice. Then I marched back to Frangipani Lodge, and into Glenn's room, bucket at the ready, eyes narrowed and breathing fire. He looked so angelic, snuggled up in his warm bed, but he was the one who had promised he wouldn't miss training, so I had no remorse.

I had been reading outback poetry to my daughters the night before, so it seemed appropriate as I emptied the frozen contents of the plastic bucket onto the sleeping swimmer, to let out a blood-curdling yell - "Heeeyaaa!!"

One Step at a Time - Glenn Buchanan

I'm not sure if it was the yell or the ice that woke him.

The deed done, I spun around towards Delaney, and spat: "You're next!"

Mean Machine member Michael Delaney promptly broke his first world record. He was up, dressed in Speedos and tracksuit, and sitting in the front seat of the waiting car in 4.86 seconds. It was a truly remarkable achievement. Glenn took a little bit longer, but he did train that day, and took his punishment like a man.

Glenn Buchanan's persistence paid off, and he had the last laugh at Los Angeles in August 1984. I saluted him on that day. The dream he'd nurtured as a young boy bore fruit because he dared to try. He dared to chase his dream. He dared to be different. He climbed the ladder slowly, one painful step at a time, never losing sight of his dream.

Congratulations, Glenn!

Chapter 5

Belief
~Jules~

The Pan Am jet touched down smoothly at Brisbane's International Airport. On board, members of the American swim team were hyped and fit, ready to race at the Pan Pacific Championships of 1987. The US squad contained many champions, but the press had eyes, cameras and microphones for only one of them - Janet Evans. Two weeks earlier this splinter-thin slip of a girl had erased Tracey Wickham's long-lived 800 metres freestyle world record from the record books. This morning the great Tracey, sporting a red-afro hairstyle to match her lipstick, was at the airport to welcome the new champ.

Tracey was polite and smiling - but feeling a little empty, a little sad. After all, she *owned* those two world records, the 400 metres and 800 metres freestyle. She remembered vividly the days on which they were set: the 800 in Edmonton, Canada at the Commonwealth Games of 1978, and the 400 in Berlin at the subsequent world championships. They'd been her personal property for nine years, and now this slimline American had come along and bowled over the longest-lasting record on the books.

Tracey elbowed husband Robert Ciobo hard in the ribs, and pointed as Janet Evans struggled through the customs arrival gates with two big suitcases.

"There she is," she whispered.

"Who, that skinny one?" asked Robert incredulously.

"Yes!"

"You sure, she looks too thin?"

"I'm sure," - a hint of impatience in her voice.

Facing page: Julie McDonald.

"You mean to say *she* broke your world record? Incredible!"

"You sure it was her?" he asked again.

"Yes Robert!" she snapped. "You don't understand ... I really wanted to keep both records till after the Olympics. Ten years would have been great ... maybe the 400 will last ten years," she mused."

"You *sure* she broke the record?" said a disbelieving Robert again, now very much on thin ice.

"Tracey, can we get a picture of you and Janet for the *Courier-Mail* tomorrow?" interrupted sports journalist Wayne Smith. Smith intervened just in time to save Robert's neck.

"Certainly," smiled Tracey. She spun away from her husband, and walked off with Wayne Smith - everybody's friend but nobody's friend - to meet the American superstar. Robert kept shaking his head. "Unbelievable," he whispered to himself. "Unbelievable!"

"Janet, this is Tracey Wickham. You broke her world record. Can we get a picture of you two together please?" asked Wayne. "Certainly!" Janet Evans replied, and turned to Tracey with a big smile and a look of genuine respect.

"Hi!" she said, in an unmistakable American accent. "I'm very pleased to meet you." "Congratulations!" Tracey said. She smiled at Janet, and kissed her lightly on the cheek. Meanwhile a voice inside her screamed, 'why am I doing this? Why am I being nice to her? This bitch has taken away part of me - she took my 800 metres world record. I wanted to hold it for ten years. Anyhow I still have my 400 metres record and maybe that will last till after the Olympics. I always thought an East German would break my records. Look at her! Robert's right. She's so skinny. How does she do it? I wonder what her strokes are like?'

"Over here Tracey!" A photographer interrupted her daydreaming. "Close together girls! Smile! Look happy Tracey! Put your arm around her. Smile! That's better! Smile! One more. That's good Janet! Big smile Tracey! Nearly finished.

Belief - Jules

*Julie (left) with Tracey Wickham, who cheered
her to victory in the PanPacs of 1987.*

Good. Closer! Closer! Last one!"

The inner voice persisted: 'I wish this jerk would hurry up
and get finished. I wonder if Julie (McDonald) can beat her? I
must ring Laurie. Yes, that's it! Wouldn't it be great if Julie
could beat her?' Tracey was dreaming again. If she couldn't
have the world record, maybe another Australian could. Maybe
Julie! "I'll ring Laurie," she said to herself.

"That's it girls, thanks!" called the photographer. Tracey
walked briskly over to her husband. "C'mon Robert," she said.
"I've had enough of this. I want to ring Laurie." She turned,
waved over her shoulder and forced a smile. "Bye Janet, nice
to meet you. Good luck!" Janet smiled shyly and waved. "Bye
Tracey. Thanks!"

Meanwhile at Chandler Pool, representatives from the electronic media had gathered to quiz Julie McDonald and me on the performances of the new superstar, Janet Evans. When they arrived, Julie was wearing her new high-top boxing shoes, bought especially for the championships. As the TV cameramen wandered into the dimly lit pool area, Julie was by the diving pool. Oblivious to approaching cameras, she was twirling a skipping rope and chatting happily to Steve Foley, the A.I.S. Coach. The television light bank clicked on and suddenly she was serious. The rope twirled at lightning speed. Skip, skip, two left, two right, front, back, repeat - she was the ultimate professional as the rope spun at breakneck speed, and her feet moved with agility befitting a world champion boxer.

A cameraman concentrated on her dazzling footwork, then flashed to her face for a quick grab. "I'm going to give her the fight of her life," she declared, directly into the TV camera.

"Great," I thought. Perhaps this was an opportunity. Julie obviously held no fears of the world record holder. She was preparing to explore limits where she had never been before. Tomorrow it would take all her tenacity and courage to go into those uncharted waters and break through new barriers. Tomorrow couldn't come quickly enough. My girl was ready to race.

Next day, Julie swam the heat and finals of the 400 metres freestyle. After being out of the race early, she finished strongly for a great second to Janet Evans. The performance gave her a real confidence boost. She knew she was swimming well.

Two days later she arrived at the pool for her favourite event - the 800. Her warm-up was methodical, planned and purposeful. Julie was savouring the bright lights, the big crowd, the uniformed swimming officials on hand for this special carnival. I walked every lap with her, not only to keep a critical eye on technique, but also to keep her mind focused on the immediate task at hand - warming up correctly. Julie was one of the most social beings imaginable in and around the pool. At competition time, when old friends and rivals arrive to compete, socialising was the order of the day for her.

On this day especially, I didn't want her chatting at the end of the pool. I wanted her totally focused on the job at hand. Warm-up finished, Julie towelled herself down, disappeared into the change rooms, donned her racing suit, and the much loved green and gold tracksuit, then came out to join me as I chatted to Australian head coach Bill Sweetenham.

"I feel great!" she beamed.

"Race her!" grunted big Bill.

"I will!" she laughed.

"See you ten minutes before marshalling," I called, happy to see she was so relaxed, so tuned in.

"OK," and she skipped off in her boxing boots. Maybe it was an omen.

"No weakness!" I screamed, as she stood behind the blocks for the start of the 800. The whistle went, signifying the swimmers were in the starter's hands. "Race her love!" I screamed even louder.

"Take your marks!" The starter barked, and seconds later the gun went.

"Go Jules!" I kept up a barrage of encouragement and cheering from my position, cramped in the Australian team section at the diving pool end of Chandler.

"Go! Go! Up! Up!" I screamed, but by now I was needing room to move. I felt claustrophobic. "Don't crack! Push! Push!" Finally, I leapt out of the seats allocated to the Australian team, and raced to the other side of the pool. I positioned myself on the pool deck next to the Americans.

This was better. I needed breathing space. I needed room to move. In the minutes that followed I stalked the pool deck at Chandler like a caged lion - ranting, encouraging, waving, gesticulating, screaming; willing Julie McDonald to victory over world record holder. As Jules inched closer to Janet my work rate increased accordingly. I was right in amongst the Americans and excitement was at fever pitch. The race was ferocious, with Evans, as was her custom, making the early

Lawrence of Australia

Coach Lawrence hustled himself into the middle of the American camp to provide the "body language" that helped get Julie McDonald home to her memorable victory over Janet Evans.

pace. At the 550-metre mark, Julie drew level and then executed a perfect tumble-turn to lead Janet for the first time. The American support team screamed louder. I stood in their midst, and matched them yell for yell.

The guts, determination, pain of training and all the sacrifices were starting to pay off. Those early-morning sessions, my insistence on quality repeats, perfect turns, on perfect finishes, on diet, the extra gym sessions, were bearing fruit. Julie that night bludgeoned the tiny American sensation into total submission.

The Americans around me were stunned into stony silence. They could not believe it. A Brisbane schoolgirl had done the impossible, and demolished their superstar. Tracey Wickham, there to see the girl who broke her world record, hardly dared believe it either. She spun around, cheered and embraced her husband Robert. Robert danced, jumped, clapped and shouted in his father's native tongue: "Bella! Bella!"

The Brisbane crowd erupted into sustained cheering. They clapped and stamped and whistled for our latest swimming heroine, a smiling, waving Julie McDonald. They gave her a standing ovation.

Janet Evans, four weeks earlier, had become an international sensation. She was front page news all over the world after she had erased the longest-standing world swim record in the book.

I looked at the scoreboard and erupted into a mixture of elation, anger, disappointment and disbelief. My Australian tracksuit that had been an encouragement banner just seconds before, as Julie pushed herself unmercifully to an historic victory, was flung onto the pool deck in disgust, frustration and disappointment, as I surveyed the time. I picked up the precious green and gold top and flung it on the ground again and again, muttering incoherently: "Missed by a whisker! Garbage! Garbage! Garbage! Damn!"

"Sit down, relax!" said Greg Lalor, the Chairman of the Queensland Swimming Association. He took my arm, tried to settle me, comfort me, calm me down.

"Congratulations Laurie! Another big win!" yelled an excited time-keeper.

I wrenched free from Greg's steadying grip, looked at the electronic scoreboard, and pelted my tracksuit on the pool deck in disgust once more. "Steady Laurie ... Relax! She's won!" he assured me.

Julie *had* won. She had broken the Commonwealth Record held by the great Tracey Wickham, but she had missed Evans' world record by a fraction of a second. The world record still belonged to the USA.

Things of value don't come by luck. They're won by pain, persistence and by sacrifices. Julie McDonald had paid the price. The victory was sweet, but she deserved better than this. I wanted the world record for her as well. I was greedy! "So close." I whispered. "It's not fair. Maybe we can get the world record in Seoul."

It's not often that one gets the opportunity or level of competition necessary to push to the limits of human endurance, to the barriers required to break a world record. That night, I was bitterly disappointed for Julie, and my emotions showed. My pre-race chat with her kept ringing in my ears: "Jules, it's better to live a single day as a lion than a lifetime as a sheep. Go after her tonight!"

"Don't worry Laurie, I am. I've got nothing to lose, she answered."

"You were swimming all over her at the end of the 400 last night," I told her. "I think you can win. Go after her tonight."

"Don't worry, I will."

And go after her she did. For Julie, her swim in the 400 metres the day before had been a turning point in confidence. After being completely out of the race at the 200 metres mark, a great second-half effort saw her come within one stroke of catching the tiny trashing machine.

The foundations were laid right there for a guts performance in the 800 metres. Australian team-mates further boosted

Julie (centre) flanked by the placegetters Janet Evans (right) and Donna Proctor after her fabulous 800 metres swim in Brisbane in 1987.

Julie's confidence by their congratulations, back-slapping, smiles and encouragement.

Confidence in sport or life is of paramount importance. I've always found that if someone believes that a job can be done, believes that something is possible, then it is so much closer to reality. It becomes easier to achieve. How many people were able to break the four-minute mile after Roger Bannister showed the way and broke four minutes for the first time? Prior to this, the four-minute barrier had seemed almost an impossible dream. Swimming times improve because as each barrier is broken, future expectations become higher.

The race over, Julie was delirious - smiling and waving and savouring the victory to the full, as pool deck officials fussed, and timekeepers checked watches. Her mother cried, her father smiled and cameras flashed. Dick Telford, Australian Institute of Sport Physiologist, extracted blood from her ear lobes for his research into blood lactate testing.

This glowing victory was a once-in-a-lifetime moment that very few athletes experience. Julie handled the media to perfection, and it wasn't until she sat down days later, and analysed her magnificent swim that she understood why I had reacted like a spoilt brat who had just been refused strawberry icecream.

"If only ... !"

"If only ... !" she muttered. "The world record could have been mine."

Now we had a young girl who really believed in her ability. The words "Seoul gold" took on a new meaning. That goal was no longer an impossible dream, no longer a slogan on a swimming cap or T-shirt, no longer the first two words used by a crazy swim coach to greet a young woman every morning at 5am. It became a tangible goal. Now Julie had a clear objective in sight: a gold medal for Australia at the Seoul Olympics.

The next 12 months would give Julie the opportunity to focus her attention on Seoul, and to set about achieving her childhood dreams. Her only limits would be those of vision. Little did we realise, at this time of jubilation and celebration, the heartbreaking obstacles that were to be encountered on the road to Seoul. It took constant determination, effort and persistence for her to fulfil her greatest dream - an Olympic medal.

The night of Julie McDonald's PanPac triumph, Steve Holland was astounded to find a 15-year-old slip of a girl crying in the shadows as he left Chandler Pool after the race.

"What's up luv?" he asked.

"I wanted to win the koala!"

"You should be happy - you won two events, and got one second."

"Yeah! But I wanted to win the koala!" she sobbed.

"You should be happy - you swam very well!"

"Yeah, but the koala was for the best swim of the meet."

"Give me your address and I'll send you a koala. Chin up luv! Keep training!"

Janet Evans kept training and Steve sent her a koala.

Chapter 6

Building a Team
~The Fishing Trip~

At the finish of the 1988 Olympic trials in Sydney, the Australian team was whisked away to train and race at Mission Bay Swim Complex at Boca Raton in Southern Florida, USA. Head coach Bill Sweetenham saw the trip to the US meet as a perfect way to mould the young Aussies together as a team.

This teamwork was accomplished as follows: all the coaching staff had agreed to make success the top priority at the Olympics. For this to happen, we had to build our young charges into a strong *team*. These young people would have to be taught that if we wanted an edge over our opponents at the Games, then we would need to work harder than them. The fact that we would all be working hard together, encouraging and supporting each other, would lead to the building of team camaraderie, and make the hard work more palatable. We needed to build up team loyalty and respect. The coaching staff agreed that if we could build a great team environment in which it was easy to train well, individual champions would inevitably emerge.

Team meetings were our means of communication. The coaches established team goals in order to keep everyone focused, and each member of the team was encouraged to set and establish individual goals. The team goal was to complement these, with the aim being to encourage everyone to pull in the same direction. Team support and praise from mates was to be the way of zeroing in on some super swims. Each team member was asked to praise good training swims by their colleagues. In this way an atmosphere was created which gave

Facing page: Sprinter Andrew Baildon provided the only highlight of the notorious deep-sea fishing excursion of 1988. He caught a fish.

every swimmer the chance of training well. Now, to get back to the story ...

At Mission Bay, ace American coach Mark Schubert controlled two crystal-clear, 10-lane, 50-metre training pools plus a large teaching pool, and an Olympic-standard diving pool. The pools were set in spacious soft green grounds fringed by waving palms. Schubert, one of America's most successful Olympic coaches, had been enticed to Mission Bay by a real estate company which wanted to use his high profile in their marketing strategies. The training and racing pools were fitted with the best non-turbulent lane ropes, and modern starting blocks. Schubert had everything a coach could need to produce world-class swimmers.

As a company promotion each year he hosted an international competition at his pool. Coaches from all over the world were invited to bring along their swimming teams, to compete and to share ideas. In a concerted effort to attract the best swimmers around, Schubert offered cheap five-star hotel accommodation, and even supplied free hire cars. American television beamed the meet live around the world.

In '88 the Aussie team raced well - in fact, we won the carnival! During the men's 1500 metres freestyle, team members lined the side of the pool, waving tracksuits in support of team-mates Jason Plummer and Michael McKenzie. This was a dedicated, totally committed Australian team. We imposed no curfew - didn't have to; the swimmers were in bed early each night. Our kids came to Mission Bay with a purpose - compete well, use the meet as a springboard to the Olympics, and get to know the people who were on their first Olympic team.

At the end of the competition the coaches and team management decided to do something special for the swimmers in recognition of the great job they had done in competition, behaviour and team support. We saw this as a positive reinforcement that would encourage the team to keep up the high standard of discipline and responsibility on future trips.

Jack Nelson, a happy character with a raspy voice who was

Building a Team - The Fishing Trip

Top: Janelle Elford - the one "survivor".
Above: Jon Sieben - in a brilliant tactical move, he missed the boat.

head coach at Fort Lauderdale, suggested we take the team on a deep-sea fishing trip, a popular pastime in Florida. I liked the idea, and volunteered to supervise the team for the day.

"Let me take them!" I enthused to head coach Bill Sweetenham.

"OK," he replied, "but leave me out! I'm not a good sailor!"

"You need me," volunteered American-born Australian coach Ralph Richards. "I was in the Navy for five years, I'll come with you!"

It was to be a five-hour excursion, fitting in perfectly with our mid-afternoon return flight. "Laurie - make sure you're at the airport by 3pm," said Bill Sweetenham. "No problem!" I replied.

I reckoned it was a terrific way to say thanks to the team for a successful fortnight of training and racing. "The word will get out how fantastic it is to be part of the Olympic team," I told the gathering of coaches. "Yep, and it's a chance for me to redis-cover my sea legs," said Ralph Richards.

The team was rapt - and particularly Jon Sieben (Olympic butterfly champion), who fancied himself as a deep-sea angler. "I reckon I'll catch the first marlin," he boasted.

I announced that the bus would leave from the hotel foyer at 7am sharp, and by 6 o'clock on the morning of the excursion the hotel was a hive of activity. Jon Sieben was first to rise. Up at 5, he zoomed around, knocking on all doors. "Marlin time! Marlin time! Wakey, wakey! Time to catch a marlin! Time to catch a marlin!" he called, as he scurried around the hotel. Jono woke the entire team early. Swimmers dragged bags, suitcases and gifts along the hallway to overcrowded lifts. Some, frus-trated by their wait for the lift, struggled to take bags down the stairwell. Boys refused to help girls. They may have been part of the team, but the standing rule was that each team member was responsible for his or her own gear.

In the foyer, big Bill Sweetenham was using his burly frame to maximum advantage - throwing bags from pile to pile, preparing them for transport from the hotel to the airport. He

Building a Team - The Fishing Trip

tossed swimming bags onto one pile, suitcases onto another and hand luggage onto yet another. His face was bright red, and beads of sweat dripped from his forehead and rolled down his ruddy cheeks as he attacked the bags with gusto. I stood and watched. Gee, he was doing a good job. I encouraged him rather than lift any heavy bags myself. Positive re-inforcement is a wonderful thing!

I emphasised to each swimmer as they brought their luggage: "Don't be late, the bus will leave at 7am sharp! Bus leaves at 7am! Not in bus, no go! No go - no catch marlin!"

Jon Sieben was like a terrier, running around snapping at heels, urging everyone to hurry up. "Don't be late, I want to catch a marlin," he urged. At 6.45am. I went out, warmed up the bus and drove it to the hotel entrance. The happy young Australian team, expectations high - laughing, chatting and giggling, climbed aboard. The carnival was over, and they were claiming their reward - we were off big-game fishing.

At 7 o'clock sharp, right on schedule, the bus roared out of the hotel car park - with one noticeable absentee ... Jono Sieben. To this day I still don't know what he was doing to miss the thing. Everyone aboard knew the standard team procedure for overseas trips: "If you are late and still want to go, get a cab. Nobody is allowed to hold up other team-mates." Sorry Jono! ... or maybe he knew something.

The team was in high spirits. As we sped along the freeway, the bus jumped to the strains of *Waltzing Matilda*. It had been a job well done, and now it was time to celebrate. We arrived at the dock, and appropriate signs led the way to where the captain was waiting on board our boat. We couldn't believe our luck. None of us had been deep-sea fishing before, and here was a magnificent vessel waiting to take us out onto the wide blue yonder.

The team was skylarking, singing, skipping and pretending to cast fishing lines. They were just like a group of Grade Threes on a school excursion. The only things missing were cut lunches and finger painting. They were rapt! The weather couldn't have been kinder. It was a glorious sunny Florida day - the sort of day you usually only see on the travel documentaries. What a morning to go fishing!

The captain was a rotund, jovial man with a hat perched jauntily on the back of his head. In a rich southern American drawl, he welcomed us on board. He explained the safety procedures and showed us other major features of the boat before we positioned ourselves out on the deck. Our deep-sea fishing boat was extremely roomy. There was one small inside cabin which had seats, toilets and small kitchen, and the entire stern of the boat had been cleared and prepared specially for fishing. Rods were positioned in cylindrical holders along the deck at regular intervals. Around the boat ran a high safety double rail, and it was against this that the swimmers positioned themselves. They were leaning over smiling, yelling, waving and laughing. It really was party time!

I felt like Santa Claus, being able to take the kids out, and give them such a fantastic day - a day to remember.

"It's nothing like the boat I cut me teeth on in the US Navy!" declared an enthusiastic Ralph.

I ignored him. "How'll it be, captain?" I inquired.

"Oh good," he said. "Once we get outside, the old girl will just roll a little bit - nothing to really worry anyone."

"I like a little swell, captain," observed Ralph. No-one heard him. We were all too engrossed. Too excited. Too wrapped up in our own thoughts.

The boat departed, and the team waved goodbye to Jono, who arrived by cab, two minutes too late. "Sorry Jono!" the team laughed.

Once out of the harbour, we buffeted through the waves for half an hour to get to the first reef. There the captain dropped anchor. "We'll fish for a couple of hours, up anchor, move on and fish a different reef for another couple of hours," he drawled. He was like a little bouncing ball as he moved among the team - handing out fishing poles and tossing smelly pilchards out of an old blue plastic bucket for bait. "Hey, the bait's bigger than anything I've ever caught," yelled Suzie Baumer, screwing up her nose as she held the pilchard up by the tail.

Now the race was on to see who could catch the first fish. "Let's get a sun tan," said Simon Upton, as he took off his shirt and started baiting his line. "We weren't allowed to take off our shirts in the Navy," commented Ralph Richards. The girls stripped to their bikinis, and got ready for some serious tanning ... meanwhile waiting for someone to bait their lines.

"OK!" I yelled. "Everyone puts in a dollar. First fish caught takes the money pool! Skins!"

Now the pressure was really on. Everyone was eager, ready to go. It's marvellous how a few dollars can motivate penniless athletes. Even Suzie Baumer started to bait her line with "that smelly thing". Andrew Baildon, the pride of the Gold Coast, was ready. He'd baited up two minutes after we left the harbour and was the first to cast his line - a long looping cast. The bait hit the water, and at the same instant a dolphin fish struck. These are magnificent fighting fish. Baildon let out a loud up-country yell.

"I've got one! Pay me! Pay me!" he shouted.

"Not until it's landed!" I shouted back. The team went wild. What a way to start - a strike on the very first cast. Baildon couldn't believe his luck as he played the big fish. Slowly he reeled the giant in until it was threshing on the water's surface.

"Get the camera!" he yelled as he landed the fish.

The atmosphere was electric. Everyone wanted to fish. Now everyone wanted to out-do Baildon. Andrew was posing, getting his photo taken, and passing the fish around to give everyone a closer look. "The fish are biting," beamed Andrew. "Like taking candy from a baby."

"We weren't allowed to fish when I was in the Navy," observed Ralph, but no one was listening ...

The Australian swim team cast out as one.

Fifteen minutes - no fish.

Half an hour - no fish.

The boat rocked gently on the southerly swell.

Three quarters of an hour later - still no fish!

The boat rocked quietly from side to side. A couple of the girls put their lines up. They were looking a bit uneasy, a little white around the gills.

Ralph Richards, Australian team coach, was giving advice, and trying to comfort some of the girls, who at this stage had lost interest in fishing. "When I was in the Navy, I found it good to keep walking the deck, and to keep taking deep breaths," comforted Ralph.

None of the girls wanted to listen, and in spite of Ralph's finest efforts over the next half hour, one by one, Australia's best swimmers began to succumb to sea sickness. I tried to make a joke of it. "C'mon fellas, no one gets seasick out here - it's a beautiful day. Buck up! Look at the horizon. Keep fishing!"

Until you've been seasick you can't really describe the feeling. The truth was I was starting to feel a bit off myself, but I wasn't prepared to admit anything to the kids. My stomach started to turn. It felt like there was a batallion of little men running around in there. I was dry retching now. At last I could sympathise with those women who suffer morning sickness. But no way was I going to give in.

"I feel great!" I called to Ralph, who was busy as a beaver now, running around comforting the girls. Some of the girls, and two or three of the blokes, had retreated inside, and were prostrate on the floor near the kitchen. They were all groaning, asking the question which I now posed to the captain:

"When is it time to go home?"

"Another two hours," he called back cheerily over his shoulder.

"Can we go back early?" I asked.

"Sorry," he replied. "We must give value for money."

"But we're happy to go back," I protested.

"Yes, but I have others to consider."

None of the Aussies wanted to stay. However, there were

Building a Team - The Fishing Trip

four American tourists on board who had paid good money for a five-hour fishing trip and who were determined to get value. It was impossible for the captain to take us home.

Ralph was like a bee in a bottle. He dashed from boys to girls, patting them on the shoulder, comforting, barking instructions: "Relax Suzie - look at the horizon! Breathe deeply Woody! Fioni, think about Australia ... don't look at the sea."

On the strength of his performance, Ralph seemed well equipped to write a book - "Ten Ways To Avoid Sea Sickness". He was great! Alas, none of his suggestions worked.

Suzie Baumer was the first to go, followed by Fioni Alessandri. This started a spate of people throwing up over the side of the boat. It was unbelievable! Within two hours these happy, smiling, laughing, singing kids were unrecognisable. Clutching their stomachs they were rushing to the port side to throw up. In between such bouts they were pleading with the captain to take them home.

Resolutely I fought the sickness. I was listening to what Ralph was saying: look at the horizon, take deep breaths, try to keep busy. I fished frantically. I must have cast my line 100 times. They talk about people who type 76 words to the minute, well I reckon I was casting that line 76 times to the minute. Apart from myself, there were only three other active Aussies left on board: Ralph the coach, darting from one to the other ("It's alright - don't be worried - you'll be right") and two swimmers, Simon Upton and Janelle Elford. Janelle was at the front of the boat, wind blowing her long auburn hair, enjoying the fresh air. Simon had his camera out, and was taking great delight in photographing people as they threw up over the edge:

"Got ya Suzie! Nice one Fioni! Smile Nicole!" he chortled. "Give us a tuna sandwich Willo!"

Then, the unthinkable happened. Ralph was a goner! From comforting one of the girls he was at the rail in 1.37 seconds flat. I've seen some people vomit in my time, but never have I seen a man put more energy into the task than Ralph. He commanded the attention of the entire boat. Even the captain came up to see if he still had his tonsils. At that point, in a vain attempt at comic relief, to get the kids' minds off their sea sickness, I started to call out to him at the top of my voice: "R A A A A L P H! R A A A A L P H!"

Duncan Armstrong couldn't resist: "Great work Ralph! Must be that Naval training. Hee, hee!" Later on, on dry land and with the miseries of that day forgotten, the catchcry that would go up in the bus, on the plane, or in the airport lounge ... anywhere, when anyone wanted coach Richards was: "R A A A A L P H! ... R A A A A L P H!"

Building a Team - The Fishing Trip

But out here, rolling on the great ocean, nothing could raise a giggle. Nothing could take young minds off the all-consuming seasickness. Meanwhile, yours truly was fighting to the last. Finally, I could hold on no longer, and succumbed to the inevitable with a quick sprint to the rail. As I was hanging over the edge, heaving my little heart out, I glanced around to see just two metres from my miserable face, our fearless, intrepid photographer, Simon Upton. Some photographers will do anything for a scoop! He was slowly closing in to get the perfect picture of "A Fun Fishing Trip".

"Smile!" he called, and clicked merrily away.

Janelle was still up front, enjoying herself. Another half hour, and every Aussie on board, with the exception of Janelle, was sick. The run to the rail had become like a relay race, back and forth, back and forth. All of us had long before given up fishing, taking up block at the rail in our favoured position. Before long I doubt there was one skerrick of food left in an Australian stomach.

The fish had a field day - there was plenty to eat, and not many hooks there to catch them. Our four American friends just laughed, and kept fishing. They wanted their five hours. Justice was done, though ... they didn't catch a single fish.

When finally it was time to head for port, the team heaved (bad choice of word here) a sigh of relief. Australia's champion swimmers were just stunned, motionless; not one word was spoken until we got back to dry land. Even then, many were still experiencing the rocking motion of the sea. We sat in a park near the pier, numb and quiet, and it was a good half hour before people started coming back to normal.

The only team member who had a good day was Jon Sieben. When he missed the boat and thus the great fishing trip, he decided to play golf with Jack Nelson. What's more, he birdied the last hole.

"R A L P H! ... R A L P H! When can we do it all again? Remember:

Always reward your charges when they do a good job!
It's good positive reinforcement.

Hmmmm.

Chapter 7

Realisation of a Dream ~The Man Who Beat Edwin Moses~

To represent your country at an Olympic Games provides a priceless opportunity to see, to meet and to talk with sporting legends. The Olympic dining hall at any Games is much more than a smorgasbord of international cuisine with an infinite variety of plain and exotic food. It provides also a smorgasbord of great athletes. Every day can offer a surprise for the avid athlete watcher. An early-morning breakfast will bring in the Kenyan athletic team, faces shiny black, sweat still on their brows from their run. At 6.30pm sharp, as if driven by clock-work, a group of young gymnasts arrives, none of them looking more than 12 years old. Rhythmically, mechanically, they pick up food trays and march in single file, ponytails bobbing jauntily. They select carefully under the watchful eye of an overweight managers, who lurks two paces behind, eyes darting from tray to tray, scrutinising each food item carefully. You know she'll be back later to eat, when her little charges are tucked safely in their rooms ...

It was in one of the many food halls at the Los Angeles Olympics of 1984 that I first laid eyes on one of my greatest idols. It was a perfect day, a day of brilliant Californian weather. I was sitting at breakfast in the open air dining room with swimmer Greg Fasala, a foundation member of the famous *Mean Machine*. The outdoor dining hall resembled a huge circus tent; marquees had been erected on the university

Facing page: Edwin Moses, the king of the 400 metres hurdles

campus to cater for hungry Olympic athletes. Cooking and eating utensils, ovens, warming trays and kitchen staff were brought onto the campus. Some of the food was cooked off-campus and transported in catering vans.

Greg and I were sipping our orange juice, starting a healthy breakfast after an early-morning training session, when into the area came gliding a lanky black athlete, of such presence that he immediately commanded the attention of the entire dining hall. He seemed almost to float, stubble on his chin, a hair line which was edging back, cool sunnies; he walked with the grace of a black panther. He stopped and looked around the hall ...

Fasala sprang to his feet and was quickly at the athlete's side. I'm not too backward in coming forward, but that day Fasala was King.

"Hey man," he said. "Come and sit with us."

"Sorry man, I'm meeting friends," was the quiet answer.

"You an athlete?" said Fasala, trying to engage him in conversation. "I'm trying to place you."

"Yeah man. I run a bit," he interrupted. "Excuse me, there's my friends."

With that he was gone, moving through the crowded hall.

"Nice try Greg," I said. "I've always wanted to talk to him."

"Edwin Moses?"

"I think so!"

As we ate we kept an eye on what he was doing and what he was eating as he chatted with his friends. I was fascinated by the man. He was so relaxed, so self-assured, so in command of the situation. Then this graceful, attention-grabbing man showed a human trait and the simple moment of humanity is burnt into my mind forever. The world's greatest 400 metres hurdler spilt part of his meal over the front of his shirt, and on the table.

Furthermore, I noticed he broke bread exactly the way we did - with his hands. Here was a man revered by millions of people around the world as a super-athlete (which he was), who ate exactly the same way that we did and who actually dropped some of his food onto the table, as all of us have no

Realisation of a Dream

doubt done. He was human, after all!

Now and then there comes a moment in a coach's life when a realisation occurs that will be of a major benefit to his young charges. That day it hit me like a bolt of lightning. This great athlete was human. In fact *all* athletes are human! And the next part of the equation is that if you're human, then you're beatable.

It was a lesson well learned - and a lesson that was reinforced strongly eight years later in Barcelona when the great pole vaulter Sergei Bubka missed his first three attempts.

I had been a fan of Edwin Moses for a long time, but from that day on, I followed his athletic career with even greater interest. I followed his 107 straight 400 metre hurdle wins - the greatest number of hurdle victories ever strung together in an athletic career. Eulogised by electronic and print media alike, he seemed invincible to athletes and spectators around the world. But from that sunny morning in Los Angeles, I knew a deep dark secret about Edwin Moses - he was human, and because of it, he was vulnerable.

In athletic endeavour, dreams and goals are the basis for achievement. Without them nothing is possible. However, dreams and goals are really only humble beginnings. They are the catalyst which motivates an athlete to pursue those dreams in order to make them a reality. The *pursuit* of the dream is more important than the dream itself. For without the pursuit, a dream can only ever be a dream, a fantasy.

Some athletes will pursue their dreams with more determination, more vigour, more purpose, more *tenacity* than others, and because of this they will reach greater success. There are countless thousands of stories around the world about athletic achievement, about the hunter and the hunted - but my favourite story among them all concerns the great Edwin Moses, and another black athlete from America, the little-known Andre Phillips.

This story of dreams and goals is really the story of Andre Phillips. We already know that Edwin Moses put together 107 straight hurdles victories - the greatest number ever - ran fast, broke world records, won two World Championships, won two Olympic gold medals. But in all the years that Moses was stringing together this fabulous achievement there was, not far away, another black athlete who also had a dream.

Andre Phillips' dream was to be the best 400-metre hurdler in the world. He coveted Moses' crown.

He wanted that crown so badly that he chased and pursued Moses like a bloodhound. He followed him around the world. He hunted him, and raced him at every opportunity. His dream was to one day beat his idol. Moses raced 10 or 15 times a year over the 400 metres hurdles. His unbeaten run stretched for almost 10 years. He won the gold medal in 1976, at the Montreal Olympic Games. In 1980 at a time when he was the fastest 400 metres hurdler in the world, world record holder, and undefeated for the year, the American team boycotted the Moscow Olympics, denying him the opportunity of another gold. In 1984, in Los Angeles, he won his second Olympic Gold medal.

The Great Man arrived in Seoul in 1988, as the colossus of his sport. But when the American flag was hoisted after the 400 hurdles final, standing on number one dais was not my hero - Edwin Moses - but the lesser known, but equally as dedicated and determined, Andre Phillips. Phillips' relentless pursuit of Edwin Moses had finally paid dividends.

As he stood on the dais, tears streamed down his face. He clutched his medal tightly to his breast as the American national anthem sounded out. Stepping from the dais, the gold medal now firmly around his neck, Phillips did not prance and dance and wave to the crowd. Instead he jogged to the side of the track. There, he stopped - and applauded Edwin Moses, allowing The Master, the man who had been king of hurdle racing for so long, to leave the arena first. It was a magnificently moving moment of sportsmanship and deep respect.

Realisation of a Dream

Footnote:

This story should be an inspiration to all young men and women who strive for athletic perfection. Imprint on your mind that athletic endeavour begins with dreams and goals. If you have no dream, no goal, you can't be there, you won't be a winner ... you have no chance of being an Andre Phillips, the man who went out and achieved the impossible. And once your goals are realised, the mountain scaled, remember then the importance of humility - just as Phillips did at the Seoul Olympics.

If you think that dreams are enough to ensure success, you are looking for the easy way. Dreams are no more than the foundation stone for success because if you don't dream of success, if you don't actualise success, it will never happen. More important than the dream is the action that follows, for without the action there can be no realisation of the dream.

Edwin Moses - the accolades are yours for what you have done for the youth of the world. There are many in the world of sport blessed with exceptional talent, but only a handful ever choose to nurture that talent to its full potential. You accomplished this, but more importantly, you were a great survivor in the gladiatorial world of athletics. You put your reputation on the line, year after year, as young men tried in vain to unseat the king. You showed many young people the value of re-setting goals. Many climb the mountain of success, but having once reached the summit, can't re-focus to repeat the feat. Your deeds will immortalise you along with Dawn Fraser, Al Oerter, and many others who have achieved success way beyond the norm.

Andre Phillips, I bow to you for your pursuit, your dedication, your bull terrier persistence. You did everything that had to be done to realise your goal.

Your true-life fairytale will inspire young athletes of all ages, of all nations, for centuries to come.

You sure you're not an Anzac?

Do it Again
Jono..

Chapter 8

Steep Roads Lead to High Mountains
~Jon Sieben~

Sport is a great leveller. It gives common man the opportunity to rub shoulders with royalty, a tradition that started as early as the London Olympic Marathon in 1908 when the Royal family requested the race start in the palace gardens.

Sport is also a great teacher. It teaches the value of dedication and commitment. Generally, in sport, if you are prepared to dedicate yourself to a goal, you will improve. In sport there are two directions: forward or backward - and the direction taken is chosen by the individual. The desire to be successful often burns in the belly of both coach and athlete, but most times the coach is merely the catalyst who provides the expertise and is the guide in helping the athlete set whatever realistic goals are required for success.

Ultimately it is the athlete who decides which path will be taken. The athlete decides whether to climb a mountain or slide down. The coach's job is to point out the reality of the endeavour; just how hard it will be. Steep roads lead to high mountains. Success becomes a choice.

I coach many young kids with gold dust in their eyes. Tough young kids with Olympic dreams. They are dreams that are shared by hundreds of other young Australian kids. They are dreams put there by the feats of modern-day champions such as Hayley Lewis and Kieren Perkins.

Of all the young swimmers I have coached over the years, no one ever attacked his Olympic dream with more intelligence or purpose than Jon Sieben. His remarkable example of

Facing page: Jon Sieben, and a pictorial memory of Los Angeles, 1984.

application, single-mindedness and toughness taught me how things *must* be done if people want to be successful - whether it be on the athletic field or in life.

Every time I watch the replay of the 200 metres butterfly final at the 1984 Los Angeles Olympics, I marvel at the barnstorming finish that brought Sieben from fifth at the final turn, more than a body length behind two world record holders, to a smashing victory. Still, I hear Mark Tonelli's call of the race:

"Jon Sieben is really challenging in lane six for a bronze or even a silver medal. So, it's Gross leading by half a body over Morales. Look at Sieben come! Third place is Vidal at this stage, and Gross is dying! They're catching him up! Sieben could be a gold medal chance here! Ten metres to go ... Sieben has hit the lead! This is gold for Australia! Three metres to go! Sieben's going to take it out! Gold for Australia! Yes, under the world record! That is a world record! Jon Sieben, seventeen years old ... that is unbelievable!"

Unbelievable? No doubt, and I ask myself the questions:

1. "Why did Jon Sieben win?"

2. "How could a 17-year-old boy who hadn't yet got the strength of a man beat Michael Gross, a superstar, a world record holder?"

3. "How could an inexperienced kid pass Pablo Morales - another world record holder?

4. "How do these things happen? Why?"

The success crystallised in Jono's win certainly didn't happen by chance or luck! Success requires planning, commitment, dedication, persistence and tough-mindedness over a long period of time. I have always insisted on the need for team work, belief and commitment. Sport is about believing in yourself, and it's about faith. Sport is about making a commitment. If you want to be successful, the answer lies in total commitment.

I have always demanded this of anyone I have ever trained either going to, or endeavouring to go to, an Olympic event.

Steep Roads Lead to High Mountains - Jon Sieben

The catch cry has always been: when your time comes to race, be ready! On the wall of the cluttered old gymnasium where we train, the message greets my swimmers daily:
"By failing to prepare, you are preparing to fail".
My hope is that the truth of this message will be etched into each swimmer's subconscious and become part of his or her battle armour. As a result, whenever the swimmers compete in an international event, they should be fully prepared, totally committed, and - once on the blocks - able to find an extra 10 per cent needed to win gold.

A sure wrecker of performance is procrastination. The question "Can I do this later?" is a certain way of *not* doing it. You can never make up missed training opportunities - and swimmers must act to protect racing confidence by completing the training tasks set by the coach.

I believe Jono won in Los Angeles not only because he was the best prepared butterflier in the field, but more importantly, he had a *mental toughness* rare in one so young. Mental toughness can't be taught or bought. When he stood up on the blocks with two world record holders in the field, he was completely unfazed. You'd have thought he had ice in his veins. He was totally confident in his ability - that confidence built by a solid preparation in which, for more than twelve months, he hadn't missed a *single* training session.

His daily routine was humdrum, but consistent: up at five daily, training in the pool from 5.30am through until 8.00am - and later if needed. During the day, seeking an edge over his opponents, he performed the extra little things. He would go for a run, or slip down to the local gym for strength training. Mid-afternoon, he'd be back at Chandler for another three-hour swim training session.

For 12 months, 11 sessions a week at the pool, and more on the road or in the gym, he kept up this daily grind. It was a training ritual he steadfastly refused to break. During the Queensland Championships, in January of the Olympic year 1984, he fell and injured an arm, and was unable to race. It would have been a disaster for many, but not Jono! Still he refused to miss training. Instead, the temporary setback was seen as an opportunity to strengthen his legs. He breezed into the pool and kicked lap after lap on a kickboard, with his arm wrapped in a fibreglass cast for protection. He ignored the taunts of fellow swimmers who teased him for missing the Championships. His mind was focused on bigger fish; with that picture clear, he kicked up and down the pool for hours.

By working on a kick which would propel him to victory in Los Angeles, he was exhibiting a mental toughness beyond his years. Jono Sieben always loved butterfly, and even as a little boy he had made it a matter of pride that he was going to be so tough that he would *never* break stroke in this, his chosen discipline. Pride and personal dignity seemed to be great ingredients for success in the world champions I coached. Jono exhibited both qualities, and no matter how hard I trained him, he was determined - as a matter of honour - that I would never crack him, would never defeat him, would never have him in a position where he would surrender to the training regime.

This eerie single-mindedness was present when he was an eight-year-old - splashing around Innisfail pool. By race day in Los Angeles, almost 10 years later, Jono had never broken stroke in butterfly. Add this to a natural competitive instinct, and you had one tough, super-confident, expectant athlete who, when he climbed up on the blocks and eyeballed his competitors, was not going to be fazed or frightened in any way by reputations.

This story is more than how a skinny little kid became Australia's only swimming gold medallist in Los Angeles. It's a story about a tough, well-prepared talented young Aussie kid who had that something extra that enabled him to go all the way. That extra factor was a quality of mental toughness unequalled by any athlete I've ever coached.

One day at the 1973 Queensland Swimming Championships at the old Valley Pool in Brisbane, a lone voice boomed across the pool warning:

"Watch the country kid in lane four! He's swallowed water! He's in trouble ... someone will have to help him out!"

It was Jon Sieben, a stringbean from Innisfail with a crew cut. He was treading water and spluttering in the middle lane as his race rivals streamed past. The leader was now some 15 metres ahead. Most nine-year-old boys in such a situation would hold onto the rope, shed a tear or two and gratefully accept a friendly hand out of the pool. Most boys would take solace from the concern expressed by well-meaning and worried officials. Most boys would appreciate the officials draping a dry towel around their shoulders, and escorting them back to

anxious parents. But not Jon Sieben. He suddenly exploded back into action and gave chase after the leaders. One by one he mowed them down - and won the race. That day, as a raw nine-year-old, he showed the promise of things to come. His courage was instinctive.

In 1984, at 17 years of age, Jono Sieben reached the pinnacle of athletic success with his victory in the 200 metres butterfly in Los Angeles. There is no doubt in my mind that four years later, in Seoul, Jon Sieben was still the greatest 200 metres 'fly swimmer in the world. Why then didn't he repeat his fantastic achievement of '84 at the 1988 Seoul Olympics? The eventual winner of the gold medal, German albatross Michael Gross, had never beaten Jon Sieben in the final of any 200-metre butterfly event. As the Seoul Games approached, Jono had the opportunity to create Olympic history by being the first man to win 200 metres butterfly gold medals back to back.

But the message on the sign on the gymnasium wall - "By Failing to Prepare You are Preparing to Fail" - was rammed home to Jono and myself on a fateful night at the 1988 Olympic trials in Sydney. As coach, I blame myself for under-estimating the opposition - and so not being totally prepared for the Seoul Olympic trials. In 1984 Jono was a hungry, aggressive 17-year-old kid. He would not compromise workouts and refused to miss training. This attitude, this hunger, was the prime reason Jono was able to climb his Everest at such a young age.

When he came back to Australia as the Olympic champion and world record holder his life changed dramatically, virtually overnight. The kid from Coorparoo, who loved nothing better than a bit of fun with the boys at Currumbin Beach Vikings Lifesavers Club on the weekends was now champion of the world and number one pin-up boy around the nation. The shy young bloke who liked a day out at the races, who liked to play the odd game of golf or basketball became an instant celebrity.

On his return he was driven down the main street of

Steep Roads Lead to High Mountains - Jon Sieben

Brisbane in an open vintage car, and presented to the people of Queensland via a ticker tape parade. In September he was feted at the Sydney rugby league grand final and the VFL grand final. Politicians fell over themselves to shake his hand. Everybody wanted him to open functions, charities chased him, organisations around the country hounded him to be their guest speaker.

The 'phone at the Sieben household ran hot from swimming clubs all over the country. "Please come and say a few words to the budding champions," they asked. In just 1min 57.04secs Jono was thrust from total obscurity into the glare of the spotlight.

This change of lifestyle was to affect his swimming performances dramatically, and my coaching performance in dealing with this new lifestyle was poor. It's easy to be wise in hindsight, but as an accredited international coach, I should have known better ... and done better. I just wasn't aggressive enough, or demanding enough of his time. My expectations of his training weren't high enough. I didn't insist he continue to do the things that made him Olympic champion.

Jono started to miss training. Often because of all these commitments, he would arrive late when he did come. As coach, I should have nipped it all in the bud. I should have tried more aggressively to make him realise that

"By failing to prepare, you're preparing to fail."

Today, whenever I see or hear the replay of Jono's 200 metres win in LA, it fills me with mixed emotions - a powerful mix of pride, joy, anger, frustration and despair. At 17 my young charge was Olympic champion and world record holder. The world was his oyster. It should have been a mere formality for him to carve a special niche in Olympic history; four years later he would be physically stronger. His mental toughness was not in doubt - that had already been displayed. By the time Seoul came around he would be in the prime of his life. There would be no stopping him.

Jono spent 1985 in the U.S.A., racing the challenging

college circuit. There in a successful campaign he demonstrated to American fans both his toughness and his quality as a swimmer.

He returned home in 1986 and his class shone through as he won both the 100 and 200 metres butterfly finals in the Commonwealth Games trials. He was off to Edinburgh. But it was about then that things started to go wrong, the beginning of two frustrating years as he prepared for the Seoul Olympics.

A severe bout of glandular fever laid him low for 12 months, and he was forced to withdraw from the Australian team. Back in the pool in 1987 he swam the PanPacs in Brisbane under great difficulties - battling badly injured shoulders. Pablo Morales beat him in the 100 metres, but Jono was still able to beat Matt Biondi home.

Surely the training run-up to the 1988 Olympics would be kinder to him? Sadly not ... the frustrations continued.

Sport, is a great leveller and there is abundant truth in the old axiom - "a rooster today, a feather duster tomorrow." Where there should have been pride and glory there is now only frustration when I think back to the lead-up to the Seoul Games.

Jono Sieben forgot how he became champion of the world. He forgot the early mornings. He didn't want to arrive at the pool at 5.30 any more ... he wanted to get there at six o'clock. But he still wanted to finish at eight o'clock - effectively cutting 20 per cent off his morning workout. He forgot the little extras he used to add to his training. The daily run was replaced by a leisurely round of golf, or a Pro-am tournament. He forgot that eight kilometres of butterfly had been a regular daily ritual - the bread and butter of his swimming diet. He forgot that before LA he hadn't missed training for 12 months, churning through 10 or 11 sessions per week, plus extras.

I had two special diver's weight belts prepared, one for Duncan Armstrong and one for Jono. Each had five kilo weights attached. Every night, as extra training, Duncan jumped into the 26 feet deep diving pool at Chandler, raised his hands above his head, and kicked for half an hour. It was a very good exercise. If you don't kick, you drown. After training, in my quest to get Jono to do more, to go the extra mile, to search for that "edge", I'd say to him:

"Jump in mate. Kick with Duncan."

"You don't need that shit Laurie," he'd say. "I've never done it before. I'll be right. "Don't worry!"

Some days he would not arrive at training until the afternoon - dog-tired from late nights, and hard living.

The conversations would go like this:

"I missed you yesterday Jono."

"Yeah!"

"Where were you?"

"I had to go down to the Coast."

"Jono, that's no good for your training!"

"Yeah it is! I did some board training. That's good for me ... and the surf was filth!"

"Jono, it's not the same as training in the pool!"

"Yeah, it's good for me. It gets me fit."

"Yes Jono, but that's an extra, not an instead of!"

"No, I think it can be an instead of. My shoulders get sore paddling the board."

"Jono, it's not the same as swimming."

"Yeah, it is. Same pulling action."

"Jono, by all means surf, but don't miss training! Don't replace swimming training with surfing"

"A little bit won't hurt Laurie."

"Jono, if you don't get first or second at the Olympic trials, you won't be going to Seoul."

"Laurie, I also need to be mentally fresh. Anyway, who's going to beat me? I've looked at the Top Ten lists a dozen times. No one will beat me. Don't panic! Once I make the team I'll lift my work rate. I want to pace it to the Olympics. I don't want to be burnt out."

Maybe I should have hit him in the mouth, made him do it. But a motivation bred out of fear or force can't last. His weight belt remained unused and the boy who was hungry for gold, the boy who was a hunter, the boy who pursued world record holders with fire in his belly, with persistence, aggression and determination, became complacent and over-confident. The hunter now became the hunted. And the bushfire that had raged within, the personal desire that had driven him to be Olympic champion, was reduced to a few smouldering embers.

The Olympic trials in Sydney arrived. The 100 metres butterfly was on the first night, and for Jono it was a breeze. He was too good, too talented, too strong - and he became the first swimmer to qualify for the Seoul Olympic team. But only two days later came his moment of truth ...

His main event was the 200 metres 'fly - the race in which four years earlier as a 17-year-old he had crushed the world's best. It is an event that requires not only courage, but also supreme cardiovascular fitness. In Sydney the elation and joy Jono felt at making the Olympic team turned sour as he struggled, half fit, into third place in the 200 final. The reality that only two per country are allowed to race each event at the Olympics hit him - his short-lived elation gave way to feelings of despair and helplessness.

I held one potential trump card. One of the swimmers who had beaten Jono had in fact scratched himself from the final after the morning heats. Under the rules he could be disqualified - if a protest was entered. I was caught in this invidious position. If I protested, the boy would be disqualified and miss the Olympic team. If I didn't my swimmer would miss the chance to defend his Olympic title. I approached Bill Sweetenham, head coach of the team for Seoul.

"No worries Laurie," said Bill. "This is like football - we need our best team out there for Australia, and if Jono can show me he's the best man for the job in six months, he'll get the nod. We want our best men in the Olympic final. The other boy will get a relay swim, so he won't come home empty-handed."

For Jono, despair gave way to hope, and I have never seen

any man train as hard as he did in the weeks that followed. He became the ultimate animal in training. In addition to endurance work, sprints, gym work and running three times a week, all team members were required to do a heartrate "set". A heartrate monitor was used to ensure that the swimmer trained and maintained a heartrate above 180 beats per minute for 45 minutes. Jono's back and shoulders would be red from the effort. At the end of it he would haul himself out of the water and lie exhausted on the pool deck, his chest heaving as he dragged in the air.

Jono Sieben was hungry again. He was now desperate to defend his Olympic title, and he was now prepared to once again pay the price. He punished his body; Jono wanted that piece of Olympic history.

The head coach scheduled closed time trials at the A.I.S. pool in Canberra prior to us leaving for the Olympics. Today I am still mystified as to why Bill Sweetenham didn't match Jono and his opponents head to head. In fact one of the chosen 200 metres 'fly swimmers didn't time-trial that event at all - but swam the 200 metres freestyle instead. Sieben's trial time was faster than he swam in a corresponding trial before the Los Angeles Olympics. Jono was ready for gold.

But it was never to be - his hopes dashed by a meeting of the Olympic swim coaches at which the decision was made that he would not swim the 200 metres - despite my protests. The agony of that decision hit me later as I sat in the stand at Seoul and watched Michael Gross win the 200 metres butterfly gold medal.

My fat Romanian friend George, a team coach, twisted the knife in an open wound when he commented: "You know, you Australians are funny people! Democracy might be alright, but we would not leave our best chance of a gold medal in the grandstand. He would be in the pool representing our country."

Time marches on and you learn from mistakes or failures or you are a fool. I learned a tough lesson at that time, a valuable

lesson: when the time comes for you to race, be ready - for nobody really cares if you were sick, hadn't prepared properly or had any one of 101 other excuses. They are too busy interviewing and taking photos of the winner! Never look for nor make excuses. Sound, basic advice for young athletes is:
- Be prepared!
- Don't compromise!
- Race tough!

As coaches or athletes we must continually re-appraise our work because the moment you forget:

1. How a champion is made, or
2. How you became a champion, or
3. The moment you under-estimate your opponents ... this is the moment you start the downhill slide.

Having been to the top with my swimmers, and witnessed the difficulties encountered in staying there has given me a greater appreciation of such people as the great Dawn Fraser. For Dawn to maintain international success as number one sprinter in the world, to be never beaten over 100-metres over three Olympiads was an absolutely incredible, superhuman performance. Dawn knew the value of a hard workout, and I've heard her expound her beliefs on numerous occasions to starry-eyed young swimmers:

You kids remember: only the pain of a hard
workout can save you the agony of defeat.

Failure, however, is only a mistake if you refuse to correct it. So let me give this advice to other young people about their athletic careers - make a big sign and put it up above where you sleep, or at your main training venue, and as you climb to the top, live by the motto:

"Perspiration is the lather of success."

Once you are at the top, make another sign and place it underneath so you are reminded daily:

"Never forget how you became good."

Steep Roads Lead to High Mountains - Jon Sieben

The fact that he was not totally physically prepared to win at the trials cost Jono the gold medal in Seoul. His application and dedication *after* the trials when he was told he had a chance of defending his gold medal was total, but being brutally frank, Jono missed too many training sessions in the lead-up the trials. That's where the damage was done. At my end I didn't put enough pressure on him to attend. I failed a coaching assignment! The teamwork was not there.

Mentally, Jono was still tough. You don't lose this quality. However, in an aerobic activity, mental practice or toughness is no substitute for physical training. Confidence can only be based on action. The harder you work in training the easier it is to race with confidence. A commitment to action is a sure way to make your dream a reality, and not a fantasy. True training commitment brings a belief in the fact that you are going to succeed. This is turn brings confidence when the moment of truth arrives. Remember:

The harder you work the harder it is to surrender.

There is another message too from the Jono Sieben experience of 1988: national coaches must remember that flexibility is an important ingredient in coaching if we don't want to throw away Olympic gold medals.

Chapter 9

Power of the Pin
~Dawn Fraser~

Some fathers are great story tellers. My dad, Stumpy Lawrence, was a beauty! He'd done a bit of fencin', a bit of bush carpenterin', even tried his hand at shearin' in a shed 20 miles out of some dry, dusty town before he found his niche - as a shearers' cook. He drew on real-life experiences to tell me stories of the bush, and of droughts. There were yarns of haggard, worked-out bush women on outback cattle stations, and of Jock, the Scottish drover, who rode a vicious, red-eyed kicker that once broke a man's leg. And stories too of dog-tired, half-caste station hands who thought nothing of riding 500 miles to have a look at the country and of Wicky Taylor, the one-eyed drover.

Most of all my dad told stories about Australia's sporting heroes. Dad loved them. He would dwell on tales of the great Don Bradman, whose legendary feats with the willow present challenges even now to today's cricketers. "He became great by perseverance and practice, son," he would tell me. He used a cricket stump, a golf ball and a water tank. You know he'd hit that golf ball against the corrugated side of the tank for hours."

Dad sang the praises of billiards champion, Walter Lindrum: "They had to change the rules to stop him, son! He'd practise 12 hours a day."

I'd sit there wide-eyed, listening and laughing for hours, demanding more stories until bedtime. And so it was as a young boy that I became soaked in Aussie sporting history and tradition, respecting and loving all our great champions, admiring their persistence and dedication.

Facing page: Dawn Fraser - en route to the Olympics and another gold medal, 1964.

Lawrence of Australia

As a snotty-nosed kid, I grew up around the Tobruk Pool in Townsville. I crabbed off the pylons on the old salt water pool and played tiggy daily after school in water that was crystal clear. I collected bottles for pocket money from the manicured buffalo grass lawns around the pool, and slept in the cramped, on-site flat above the pool foyer, between the ladies' and gents' dressing sheds.

There, I witnessed the golden era of Australian swimming and was privileged to rub shoulders with members of the Australian swimming teams of the period 1956-1964. Jon Henricks (1956 Olympic 100 metres freestyle champion, and the first man to shave all the hair off his body to race), lived with us in that little flat whenever he was in camp with the Australian team.

Jon Henricks (centre), the 1956 Olympic 100 metres champion, helped ignite a passion for the sport of swimming in the young Laurie Lawrence. With Henricks in Ern McQuillan's classic photo are Murray Rose (left) and John Devitt.

Power of the Pin - Dawn Fraser

Once in a lifetime there steps onto the sporting arena a genius, a special talent; a sportsman or sportswoman who stands head and shoulders above all the others; a sportsperson ahead of his or her time; a champion whose feats become legendary. Such a person became a confidante of my father, and he became her personal masseur whenever she was in Townsville. I became her greatest fan.

This champion of champions broke 39 world records, and along the way:

- Won the most medals by an Australian at the Olympics (8).
- Won the most gold medals by an Australian at the Olympics (4);
- Was the first woman to break 60 seconds for the 100 metres freestyle.
- Held the 100 metres freestyle record for 15 years.
- Was undefeated from 1956-64 at that distance.
- Won the Olympic 100 metres freestyle championship at three consecutive Games.
- Still held the world record eight years after her forced retirement.

She was, of course, the incomparable Dawn Fraser. Dawn helped shape my love of swimming and I've loved her ever since I was a starry-eyed kid chasing her around the Tobruk Pool, hunting autographs. She never refused, even though I asked her daily. I got her to sign scraps of paper, old pro-grammes, newspaper clippings, T-Shirts, and even my arm - so I could skite to the kids at school.

"Your signature please, Dawnie! Oh! and could you sign this one for Eddy?" "There y'are mate!" was always her cheerful reply as she scribbled away. Nothing was ever too much trouble for that Great Lady. I even followed her down to Bluey Raleigh's old pub on the strand, where, after training, she would often sit and relax in the unpainted lounge bar, sinking a couple of cold pots and swapping yarns with Bluey.

No wonder I cheered when she won the Olympic 100 metres freestyle golds in Melbourne, Rome and Tokyo - an achievement unlikely to ever be repeated. No wonder I was shocked, and cried openly, when she was suspended by the Australian Swimming Union in 1964 for alleged events at the Tokyo Games, including attempting to swim the Emperor of Japan's moat to souvenir a flag.

It was 20 years later that I realised a boyhood ambition. I placed five swimmers in the 1984 Australian Olympic team, and was selected as one of Australia's coaches to take the team to Los Angeles. I was on cloud nine!

The Olympic village was on the campus of the University of Southern California. We soon discovered it wasn't exactly the plushest part of Los Angeles - and all Australian team members were warned not to leave the village, especially at night. The security was especially strict. Armed, uniformed guards patrolled the rooftops like soldiers on the old Berlin Wall - their machine guns in full view. The only difference was that the US version smiled and talked if ever you got close enough.

On our daily training trips to training pools out of the village we went by bus. Management and swimmers would press their noses against the windows straining for a better view. It was certainly not upmarket Beverley Hills. Many of the buildings were old, unpainted and rundown. Black, Hispanic and white youths walked the streets, looking for something to do. The area represented very much the lower end of the socio-economic scale. It was not a place to travel alone, day or night. After one early-morning jog with coach John Rodgers, I made up my mind to stick to the in-house movies supplied for us in the village.

The great Dawn Fraser was in LA for the Olympics as a guest of the press. She was staying in a hotel three kilometres from the village, along with other members of the Australian press contingent. The hotel was five star, built especially for the Olympics - and completely out of touch with the surrounding suburbs, with their sleazy streets and dilapidated buildings.

Power of the Pin - Dawn Fraser

Since Dawn was always great value to "rev up" the kids with a pep talk at team meetings, head coach Terry Buck brought her into the village to share an evening meal with the team, and give a few words of advice and encouragement to our young Olympic hopefuls. Terry figured maybe Dawn would say something that would click with the younger brigade, giving them the little "edge" they needed against our more fancied opponents.

Just before Dawn began speaking that night, the Italian basketball team, housed one floor above our girls' team dormitory, moved loudly into the Olympic spirit, singing Italian songs, and bouncing their basketballs on the ceiling in an impromptu game. Dawn's patience was quickly exhausted. She couldn't speak under these trying circumstances so she decided to do something about it.

She spun on Terry Buck: "What's this sh— Terry?" she asked. Buck explained the problem: "The management have tried, Dawn, but no luck," he said. "These bloody 'Ities' just bang their balls on the roof all day and half the night. And if they sing 'A rev ya duck to Roma' one more time I'll spew!" "We can't sleep," squealed a couple of the younger girls (who thought the one with the curly hair was cute). "The tall one thinks he's Jose Carreras," giggled another.

"Leave it to me," said Dawn. "I swam in Rome. I know a bit of 'Itie'... arriverderci!!." With that she was off, striding from the room, up two stairs at a time - to confront the entire Italian basketball team, on her own! I looked at Terry Buck: "We'd better go help her, Terry," I said.

"Dawnie doesn't need help," said Terry. "I've seen her in action before ... but we'll go along as a backstop." We were 10 paces behind and hurrying - but Dawn was already in full flight. There is something about a champion which commands attention. She burst into the room, yelling in fractured Italian: "Bambino!"...

Her translation of what she said went something like this: "No more bouncing!"

"No one can sleep!"

"You pasta-eating bastards!"

"Bounce again, and I'll push this ball up your ——!"

You could have heard a pin drop as Dawn spun on her heel and strode out. The Italians were stunned into silence. They couldn't believe their eyes, or ears. With a few well-chosen words a woman had controlled the whole team. But this, of course, was no ordinary woman. They had run up against one of those rare individuals who believed in action, and who actively lived the slogans "don't put off till tomorrow what you can do today" and "don't procrastinate." This was a woman who believed all things possible with faith, action and persistence. Dawn Fraser lived, and lives her life by, those principles.

Power of the Pin - Dawn Fraser

When Dawn returned to the meeting, she was greeted with an enthusiastic and spontaneous standing ovation from the young Aussies. It would have matched any ovation she received for her Olympic victories. She beamed, and started her talk ...

"Remember, always be in charge when you race," she told them. Don't let anyone intimidate you." She was great. Within five minutes she had the kids eating out of her hand. Her frankness and knowledge of the Olympics and the messages she preached put them into a fantastic winning frame of mind. Her stories of past Olympians, though embellished as only Dawn can, entertained the young Australian team mightily. They could hardly wait to compete. She talked of the fun of competing, the joy of doing your best, the value of domination and confidence, the adrenalin buzz of head-to-head competition, the importance of self-control, and of the exhilaration of victory. It was positive reinforcement at its best; no psychologist could have done better. It was the perfect pre-Olympic talk, a masterstroke by coach Buck.

After a few more stories and a few more laughs, Dawn begged to be excused - but not before she had conned a kangaroo pin from every member of the team. I requested permission from Terry to escort her back to her hotel, and we headed off into a gloomy night.

There was no moon or stars, and the sky was pitch-black when she turned the hired Ford station wagon into the narrow alley which led to the dimly lit car park situated at the back of her hotel. "Perfect night for a mugging," I joked. The headlights promptly flashed onto a group of youths loitering in the car park, five of them. A cigarette glowed, as one drew deep. "Oh shit!" I gasped, then remembered Dawn's words from the talk: "Always be in charge when you race, don't let anyone intimidate you."

"Leave them to me," said Dawn, cool as a cucumber - and she parked the car right where the youths were gathered. By this time I'd just about filled my pants! "Hi guys!" said Dawn,

Lawrence of Australia

Dawn and Laurie - best of mates.

as she bounded out, and locked the car.

"Aussies!" they exclaimed, recognising her unmistakable, broad accent. "Sure. We've come from Down Under to this great country of yours for the Olympics." "No shit, man!" said the youth holding the cigarette.

"That shit'll kill ya man!," said Dawn to the smoker, picking up the street lingo in an instant - a relic of her Balmain days. "Hey! This chick's cool!" said one of them.

With that Dawn seized the opportunity. She marched up and planted a kangaroo pin (conned from our kids) on the shirts of each one of the five. "Here, have one of our Aussie Olympic kangaroo pins," she said. "Thanks, man. No one's ever given us pins before!" beamed a black youth sporting long dreadlocks. "No problem! We're Aussies! You guys know *Waltzing Matilda*? Sing for them, Laurie!"

With this, she gave me an enormous prod in the ribs, and I burst into song. Now, I'm something of an amateur entertainer, and I love it, but this was a bit much. I was in fear of my life. "You're a bit off key, man," said a youth with torn shirt, torn jeans and top-of-the-range Reeboks. "You do better, man!" retorted Dawn, to my horror. I now had clear visions of us being mugged.

I needn't have worried. He broke into a rendition of *Waltzing Matilda* that would have made John Williamson proud and the others joined in the chorus.

Within two minutes Dawn had these guys eating out of her hand. For the next 20 she taught them a bit of good old Aussie slang. She made one of them "pull his finger out" and go and get a dozen stubbies so we could all "sink a coldie" together. When he came back, we had to sit in a circle, and Dawn conducted an Aussie-American singalong. I nervously recited Banjo Paterson's *Man From Ironbark* to the cheers of Dawn and her new pals.

Finally, we said farewell. Once inside the hotel, I collapsed on the downstairs lounge in nervous exhaustion. Dawn patted me gently on the shoulder. "See ya in the morning, mate. I'm off to bed!" It took me an hour to get control of my adrenalin rush, and be relaxed enough to get a cab back to the village.

"Anything exciting happen, Laurie?" yawned Terry Buck, as I let myself into the coaches' unit. "Terry, you wouldn't believe it. It's too long a story," I said. " 'Sides, I need to wash out my undies ..."

Next morning at Dawn's hotel, all hell broke loose. Four car-loads of heavily armed and uniformed police arrived from the Los Angeles Police Department. The duty sergeant summoned Dawn to the hotel manager's office. "Repeat your story again please, Miss Fraser. What time did you come in? How long were you in the car park? I find it very difficult to understand that of the 38 cars in the carpark, yours is the only one that hasn't lost all its wheels!"

"Sergeant, never underestimate the power of an Aussie Olympic pin," she said with a mischievous glint in her eyes. With that, Dawn leant across and pinned a golden kangaroo onto his shirt-front.

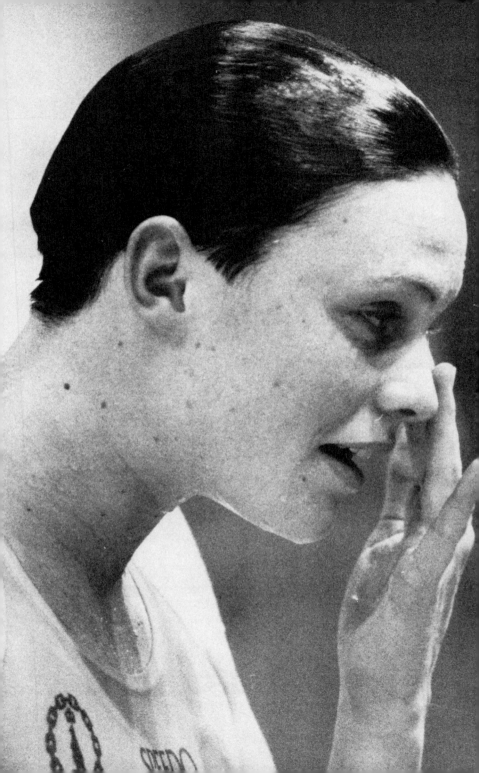

Chapter 10

Drastic Steps
~Julie McDonald~

The Australian sporting media live by simple rules not unlike the ones prized by the Gladiators in ancient times: "Win and you're in - lose and you're out". You could call it the thumbs-up or thumbs-down attitude to sport.

Julie McDonald was the darling of the Australian media after her magnificent win over the USA's world record holder Janet Evans at the Pan Pacific Games in Brisbane in 1987. Julie, the bubbly Queensland distance swimmer, sometimes suffered from "foot in the mouth" disease (similar to her predecessor Tracey Wickham), and, after a number of below-par performances, had fallen from favour with the Australian media. The media rated her then as only an outside chance to make the Seoul Olympic team. Fifty to one was the quote, in fact.

The summer of 1987-88 was a frustrating one for Julie. Her training punctuated by a series of injuries and viruses, it was impossible for her to be at peak fitness. Additionally, she was a few kilos above her racing weight. Under these circumstances, and despite being physically well below her best racing form, Julie attended the 1988 Summer National Championships, determined to give it her best.

Dick Caine, swimming coach, larrikin, garbo, trotting trainer, odd-job man extraordinaire from Carss Park in Sydney and the man who had put Michelle Ford on the 1976 Olympic team as a 13-year-old, had Janelle Elford in perfect physical and mental shape for the titles. Janelle, superbly fit, smiling, aggressive and hungry, thrashed Julie in every event at the Nationals.

Lawrence of Australia

The press now had a new heroine. Janelle's efforts were outstanding, and ranked her among the world's best. She was hailed as the number one Australian contender for Olympic honours.

Poor Jules. Six months earlier *she* had been the heroine, the darling of the Australian media, the Olympic medal contender. Now she was categorised as being of historical significance only, and in real danger of missing the Olympic team. In fact, most of the sports journalists had already written off Julie as an Olympic representative.

Julie read the various newspaper reports, bit her bottom lip, and fought back tears of frustration and anger. She knew what was required to make the team. How quickly they forget, she thought. After all, she still held the Commonwealth 800 metres freestyle record.

"They give me no credit, Laurie," she cried one morning.

"I know, Julie. It's sad."

"Why?"

"The cold hard facts of life are that once you achieve high standards, you become public property. They expect you to perform at that standard all the time. If you don't, then the press and the public look for a new heroine. Sports heroes are expendable in Australia, just as the Christians were in ancient Rome."

"But we've got feelings too!"

"I didn't say I agreed," I offered ...

"What I've done counts for nought?" she interrupted.

"It counts to you Julie, in terms of personal achievement," I replied. " But if you don't perform at the Olympic trials, I'm afraid you will be watching the Seoul Olympics on TV. You are only as good as your last performance."

"I want to be in that team," she answered with strong conviction.

"Good. You've set a goal. That's a start."

"What's next?"

"We analyse what's required to make the team."

Drastic Steps - Julie McDonald

"And then?"

"We do it! We work with more guts and more determination than we've ever done before. Are you prepared to pay the price?"

Her answer was a simple but resolute "Yes!"

"Good, then let's go for it," I replied happily, knowing I had a committed athlete. "Here are our positive steps: first made a list of your goals; then make a list of anything you think is limiting your performance. Bring them back to me as soon as you've finished and we'll make further plans."

The stage was set for an absorbing battle to make the Olympic team. The journos hadn't counted on the determination of a couple of hard-nosed Australians who perform at their best with their backs to the wall.

A hurried analysis of the National swimming results on the late plane back to Brisbane showed Julie and I that drastic action was definitely needed if she was to make the Olympic team.

Once home, I couldn't sleep. Restlessly I tossed and turned. I had nightmares of Julie missing the Olympic team, and I knew she had dreamed of going to the Olympics for her country ever since she was a little tot. I remembered how she had swum the length of my teaching pool at Slack's Creek to show her older brother Darren just how tough she was, and to prove to her mother Royalle that she should have lessons at Laurie Lawrence's Swimming School as well.

Finally, at 3am, I got up and penned my thoughts on the back of an old swimming programme; thoughts to help Julie and all my Olympic aspirants.

1. Blood test - tight check on health.
2. Time all repeats. Important to keep record!
3. Racing weight. Check daily!
4. Dietitian - Henry Osiecki.
5. Work guts out!
6. Be positive towards each other.
7. Be positive towards swimmers as their coach, and praise when due.

8. Supervise stretching. Don't be lazy!

9. Keep team moving. Minimise chatter.

10. Better warm-ups.

Julie probably didn't think my reaction would be as immediate or as drastic, but at 4am the day after returning from the unsuccessful National Championships, on a cold and pitch-black Brisbane morning, I rattled the sliding glass door at the McDonald's house in Rochedale. I was greeted by Mishka, Julie's Australian cattle dog, an overfed blue heeler which obviously had never chased a cow in its life, but a good guard dog anyway.

"Sshh Mishka, it's only me. Don't bark! Don't bite! Nice dog!"

"Shut that dog up, Royalle!" bellowed Julie's dad.

"Yes Harold," Royalle replied sleepily.

Mishka, behind the glass door, was going crazy. My leg must have looked very tasty! Thirty seconds later, Julie's mum arrived, bleary- eyed, in her dressing gown."What the bloody hell are you doing here so early?" was her enthusiastic good morning greeting.

Drastic Steps - Julie McDonald

"I've come to walk to the pool with Jules. I want her to trim down a little," I replied.

"Are you mad? It's bloody freezing out there, and she still hasn't shaken the virus that's plagued her all summer. I want her in the team - not in the hospital, Laurie!"

"Fair go Royalle! Wake her up! Be sensible and wake her up! Come on Royalle, be reasonable," I pleaded.

"Jules, it's Laurie," she called over her shoulder.

"What time is it?"

"Four am"

"What!!"

"I told him you still had the virus, but he won't listen!"

"Tell him to walk himself, today. I'll go with him tomorrow." She refused to budge.

Furious, I walked to the pool on my own, and arrived half an hour late for training - the walk from Julie's to Chandler had taken a little longer than I anticipated.

I was filthy. The squad was working solidly as I strode angrily into the pool area. "Morning, Laurie. Little late?" taunted Duncan Armstrong. "Shut up, Armstrong!" I spat.

No one else dared speak.

I slumped down on the pool deck, scowled, and scrutinised every little detail, daring someone to make a mistake. I was desperate to take out my frustrations on some poor unsuspecting swimmer. My assistant coach, Ian Findlay, efficiently put the squad through their paces, an 8,000-metre workout. They worked like clockwork. Lap after lap, turn after turn, dives, sprints, kicks - all were perfectly executed. They were highly motivated young men and women - their gazes turned towards the prized green and gold blazer. The Australian Olympic swimming trials were eight weeks away, and every lap, turn, dive, time and sprint was vital.

I repeated the 4am early morning ritual at the McDonalds' for the next week, even though it did seem a little early to go visiting friends. By the end of the week, I was becoming quite cranky. I'd walked 60 kilometres, and hadn't had Julie as a walking companion once. What's more, my early-morning visits were becoming distinctly unpopular in the McDonald household. Mishka was now the only one giving me a rousing reception. I was starting to appreciate the Roy Orbison hit song *Only the Lonely*.

I never once asked Julie why she wasn't coming; I just kept arriving at her doorstep every morning at 4 o'clock, hoping Mishka couldn't get through the glass door. I only found out by accident that Julie was deliberately letting me do the early-morning walk on my own. She slept in for the extra hour, while I walked in the dark, then in the middle of the day, she would do an hour of work on her own: a private circuit of skipping, sit-ups and arm work.

"Let the silly old 'B' walk alone, it'll do him good," I overheard her say to Jono Sieben after training one morning.

"Don't you think you should tell him?" Jono chuckled.

"Nah, he prides himself on being so tough," she joked. Then she thought out loud: "Maybe I should let Mishka out one morning."

"Don't do that!"

"Why not?"

"Well," said Jono, "as it is, he already gets here all sweaty and in a filthy mood after running from your place, and takes it out on us. Imagine what he'd be like if he was chased by a dog as well."

"Mishka wouldn't bite him. I'll keep doing my own mid-day circuit for a couple more weeks. If he doesn't wake up by then I'll tell him."

Poor old coach ... sucked in again! I'd been upset with Julie for not being totally committed to making the Olympic team, but unbeknown to me she had been working and doing twice as much as I had ever expected of her.

Next morning, I slept in.

zzzzzzzzzzzzzz ... thank God!

I slept peacefully in the knowledge that at the Olympic trials I would have a fit young swimmer ready to race, a young

Drastic Steps - Julie McDonald

girl who was leaving nothing to chance in a desperate battle against time - determined to realise her dream of winning the honour of being called an Australian Olympian. Julie had formulated a plan and was now sticking rigidly to it. She now had a chance of success. I felt great. As a coach, one can only do so much; at some stage the athlete must take some responsibility for part of their training. Motivation starts from within, and self-motivation is the tool of victory.

There were now only eight weeks to go. I played my part, and religiously attended to all the various little details of times, distances and programmes. I planned and re-planned, leaving nothing to chance in an all-out effort to give my swimmers the best possible chance of making the Olympic team, and knowing that:

By failing to prepare you are preparing to fail.

Julie also played her part with total dedication. One day she arrived with her list of goals. They were:

1. Lose excess weight.
2. Win Open Nationals (team).
3. Make Olympic team
4. Win gold medal 800 metres freestyle in Seoul.
5. Win medal in 400 metres freestyle in Seoul.

The things I have to do to achieve goals:

1. (a) Do more than everyone else.
   (b) Eat less.
   (c) Eat right foods.
   (d) Run and skip.
2. Train harder than everyone else.
3. Do my best in training.
4. Make training fun, and enjoyable for myself and everyone else.
5. Do my 6-10 kilometres quickly.
6. Do everything right.
7. Be positive.
8. Work "little things".
9. Race the guys.

10. Beat the guys.
11. Be competitive in training.
12. Don't leave any stone unturned.

The things I'm doing to achieve my goals:
1. Doing more extra things than everyone else.
2. Cutting down on food intake, and watching weight.
3. Running three mornings.
4. Skipping three mornings.
5. Trying my best in training.
6. Encouraging others on efforts in training.
7. Working turns and trying to improve them.
8. Racing people in training.
8. Being competitive in training.

The things limiting my performance:
1. Over my ideal racing weight.
2. Not as strong as the men.
3. A few negative thoughts creeping in.
4. Feeling tired during training (could be from extra work and weight.)
5. Need of encouragement.
6. Disappointed in swimming slowly in training.
7. Difficulty in motivating myself.

With these problems identified, we could attack problem areas. Eight weeks flew by and the day before the trials the Queensland team headed for Sydney. Expectations were high.

The following morning Julie swam in the heats of the 400 metres freestyle. Her stroke was smooth and rhythmical. She bounced along the surface of the pool like a dolphin at play, loping effortlessly to the easiest win of her career. Sometimes in sport, all things click. You hit the golf ball with perfect precision, or bowl the perfect lawn bowl. You reach that moment in time where great athletes seem to make sport look easy. For Julie, this was it. She was the fastest qualifier, and after her swim she came back elated.There was no doubt she was HOT!

"I feel great. Tonight just you watch out for Julie McDonald

Drastic Steps - Julie McDonald

Julie's fighting spirit brought her back to win an Olympic medal in Seoul, 1988.

in the final. I'm going to kick a few heads, and I can't wait!" she announced. "Great, Jules!" I enthused.

As coach, I was ecstatic. I skipped, shadow-boxed, and slapped any fellow coaches who were within easy reach on the back. Some who weren't within easy reach got a little touch-up as well. You would have thought it was the final. The little master coach had done it again. What flair! What ability! What a genius! Eat your heart out, Forbes! My head, people were saying, was slightly swollen.

That night the swimmers on our team started sensationally. Jono (Sieben) broke the Australian record for 100 metres butterfly, and was the first Australian swimmer selected in the 1988 Australian Olympic team to Seoul.

Lawrence of Australia

I could hardly wait for Julie's event. Soon enough the spotlight was on the women's 400 metres freestyle and she was behind the blocks, her usual bubbly self - talking to other swimmers, and joking with the timekeepers. She was confident and ready.

I sat smugly in the stand, twirling my stopwatch. Three times left, three times right, twice left, twice right. Not a worry in the world, just sitting there waiting for my next swimmer to cruise into the Olympic team. The starter's gun exploded my daydreams. The Olympic hopefuls were off to a good start.

By the time the field had gone 100 metres, I knew there was something horribly wrong. Gone was the easy rhythm which Julie demonstrated in the morning heats. At the 200-metres mark, she was really struggling, fighting to stay in touch with Janelle Elford and Sheridan Burge-Lopez. It was obvious even at the halfway mark that she was beaten. I just couldn't believe it! My mind raced.

"Why? Why? Why?"

Head coach Bill Sweetenham passed by, winked and smiled, and nudged me in the ribs with his elbow. "Cunning move, Laurie," he said. Saving her for the 800 metres, eh?" "Yeah. Sure Bill." I stared blankly ahead, stunned.

At the end of it, Janelle and Sheridan were jubilant.

And I was a worried man. By the look on Julie's face she was more than worried. Five seconds worse than her heat time! What had gone wrong? She was devastated. However, I rationalised, a real champion will always lift himself or herself in tough situations, lift out of the depths of despair and fight. A real champion is someone who gets up and fights when under extreme pressure, who digs deep into their athletic reserves and who thrives on pressure.

Julie McDonald was now clearly under pressure. Over in the warm-down pool she was at a loss to explain her disappointing performance. I was trying to retain a positive attitude, and not show her my anxiety, which could have a disastrous effect on her performance. The words of Dale Carnegie kept spinning through my mind:

The successful man will profit from his mistakes, and try again in a different way.

I immediately focused her thoughts towards the 800 metres, knowing that once an athlete has a clear objective, often he or she will unleash their inner power which will then make it easier to achieve that seemingly impossible dream.

"I'm not totally unhappy with the result, Jules," I lied. "It will give us a better chance to concentrate on the 800 metres in Seoul"

"Yeah, but I'm not even in the team yet," she answered dejectedly.

"A mere formality, kid. You'll kill 'em tomorrow! You've done the work. You know you have planted the seeds! You only have to harvest the crop tomorrow. You're swimming well. You only need a good night's sleep now. See ya in the morning!"

After the team had been bedded down, veteran coach Forbes Carlile, who sleeps very little anyway, got a very late-night phone call. "Forbes, I'm desperate for a portable VCR and the tape of Julie beating Janet Evans in the Pan Pacific 800 metres last year."

"No problem," said Forbes. "Pick it up in the morning at Killarney Pool."

"You sure?"

"Yeah, ask John Coutts, he'll organise it."

"Thanks Forbes," I said gratefully.

Good old Forbes, a pioneer of Australian swimming and the sort of bloke you could always count on in a crisis. I felt comfortable in the knowledge that I now had the ammunition to give Julie a psychological lift before her battle to make the Olympic team. It would be a race in which she would need physical endeavour. Was she willing to pay the price? Could she handle the pressure?

Early the next morning we met at the pool for a wake-up swim and it was during this valuable time that I worked on

Jules' stroke technique: analysing, refining, fine-tuning the hand entry, the hip rhythm, the head position - until she felt the smooth easy power which comes when stroke technique is perfect.

"You look great, Jules!" I enthused, pouring out the positive vibes. "I'll see you after lunch. I'm going to stay here for the morning heats. Bye." "Bye," she called as she walked out, not only contented but now with real purpose in her step.

At the end of the morning heats, and after I had dropped a couple of my swimmers back to their motel, my thoughts turned to Julie and to the 800 final. I headed for the McDonalds' flat overlooking the water at Manly; a little mental boost, a top-up over lunch wouldn't hurt her, I decided.

"Hi Royalle! Where's Jules?" I asked.

"In her room," replied her worried-looking mother.

"Don't worry Royalle, she'll do it. " With that I marched towards Julie's room.

Nothing could have prepared me for the surprise I encountered as I burst into the room. There she was lying flat on her bed like an Indian Swami, her eyes closed, and breathing deeply. Standing at the foot of her bed was my little dietitian mate, Henry Osiecki, monotonously droning: "Sleeeeep! Sleeeeep! You will sleep deeper than you have ever slept before. Sleeeeep! Sleeeeep!"

I was horrified. This was my expert on *nutrition*. The guy I'd approached to watch her diet, to help her lose weight and to encourage her to eat celery, carrot sticks, and lettuce leaves, and to advise her on her vitamin intake. Now he had taken it upon himself to branch out and try a little hypnotherapy. I wasn't only horrified, I was bloody furious.

"Piss off Henry!" I growled.

"Shhh. Now wait a minute Laurie."

"Piss off Henry!" I repeated, furious now - and with that shouldered him straight through the open doorway and out of the flat. I returned quickly to a now wide-awake and startled Julie.

Drastic Steps - Julie McDonald

"You don't need that garbage!" I snapped at her.

"But Henry ... " she stammered.

"The only person who can help you now, young lady, is YOU. Y -O- U. We're playing for high stakes, and we're playing to win."

At that moment there appeared on the scene Brian Smith, Australian rugby representative, subsequently star rugby league halfback with Balmain. Brian, a friend of the McDonald family, dropped by to wish Julie all the best in the final. It couldn't have happened at a more fortuitous moment.

"Smithy," I said. Take her for a walk on the beach. Talk rugby, movies, drugs, politics, or sex. Anything but swimming."

"No problem," said Brian. C'mon Jules!"

Laughing, they headed for the beach, while I flopped in the lounge chair, tired and mentally drained. Tonight was going to be a super challenge for coach and swimmer alike.

That evening I was the first swimming coach at the pool. I signed in, then rigged Forbes' VCR up in the small ambulance room just off the pool deck. I fast forwarded the tape to the crucial turn where she overtook Evans at the Pan Pacific Championships. It was now set and ready to go at the flick of a button. Julie warmed up automatically, meticulously.

I was up and down the pool, rounding up my swimmers like a good kelpie. I oozed confidence, knowing that the greater the belief one has in his or her capacity to achieve a goal, then the greater the success rate. I had to have Julie believing in her ability to win the race, to be confident and not to panic. I worked on her technique and pace work right back to the fundamentals.

She was physically ready, needing only a mental top-up now. I hoped the video would achieve this.

"Meet you in the first aid room in 10 minutes, Jules."

"Why?" she asked, perplexed.

"Don't ask why, just be there!" I pressed. "I want to show you something."

Ten minutes later she walked in, dressed and ready to race. I picked up the Oxy-Viva, kept in the room for emergencies, and showed it to her. "Royalle might need this tonight!" I said. We both laughed. She was relaxed now, and that was great.

"Watch this!" I said, and switched on the VCR.

Jules looked on in silence, re-living her demolition of Janet Evans at the Pan Pacific Championships in Brisbane.

"Do you think any of the girls you're racing could beat Janet Evans?" I asked her.

"No!" she snapped.

"Do you want to give these Australian sheilas your ticket to the Olympic Games?"

"No!" she snapped again.

"Are you going to let them take your ticket?"

"No!!!" - even more emphatic this time.

"Well Jules, Olympic selection is today. You've done the work, and I can't help you any more. Henry can't help you with his mumbo jumbo. Your mum and dad love you, but they can't swim for you. It's up to you. And remember, these girls want *your* ticket."

"They've got no chance," she said.

Julie was ready to take pressure head on. The improvement she showed that night was dramatic, and although not up to the lofty standard of her magnificent Commonwealth record, she swam a great race to take the silver medal behind Janelle Elford, and thus get the nod from the Australian selectors for a swim in the 800 metres in Seoul.

After the race she came back beaming."Thanks," she bubbled, and skipped away to celebrate. She stopped after about ten paces, turned, flashed a smile and called back:

"Don't worry! I'll get her in Seoul."

"Only if you work hard!" I tossed back, not wanting to miss an opportunity to plan for the future. The gauntlet had been thrown down for an absorbing duel in Seoul. Julie was hungry and confident again. The competition would be greater in Seoul, but it's a truism of sport that the tougher the competition, the sweeter the victory.

Julie went on to prove her point in Seoul. There, she was Australia's only female medallist, winning a magnificent bronze medal behind Janet Evans. Julie's medal came after a fantastic battle with two East German swimmers for the minor placings. Astrid Strauss, the girl who beat Julie for the silver, was later suspended for a steroid offence.

Chapter 11

Champions Come in all Shapes and Sizes
~David Berkoff~

I flashed my precious Olympic ID to two Korean security guards, tipped my Akubra and hurried downstairs, anxious for my first close-up inspection of the Seoul Olympic Pool. Meanwhile, the other members of the Australian team of 1988 were settling into the high-rise unit blocks that were to be home to 370 very proud Aussies for the next couple of weeks. Swimmers, shooters, athletes, yachtsmen, basketballers, weightlifters, boxers, doctors, physios, masseurs, coaches, administration staff - among others - had gathered as a team, striving for sport's great prize, an Olympic medal.

I couldn't wait. I just had to get out and inspect the racing venue. I wanted to soak up the Olympic atmosphere; I needed to be completely at home, totally comfortable with the surroundings when my swimmers arrived. I wanted to exude confidence to them. I had to have them believe that this pool was going to give them the opportunity to display their talents and fitness to the world. The persistence and dedication that they had shown in becoming Australian Olympians would be fruitless if they could not go on and achieve their "personal best" results here.

Historically many notable winners have encountered heart-breaking obstacles, and overcome many defeats. These sort of people push on against pressures that seem insurmountable at times; by sheer persistence (a quality shared with our early Australian pioneers), they triumph.

Lawrence of Australia

Many of my young Olympic charges were now on the brink of realising their goals. "I must help them," I thought. "I must give them stability, reassurance and confidence. I must give them a stable platform on which they can build a super performance. The hard work had been done over 12 long months, we must not be mentally brittle now."

Preparation was about to meet opportunity.

Once downstairs past the grim-faced security guards, I strode halfway along the beautiful 50-metres warm-up pool. It was already seething, alive with finely-tuned, beautifully proportioned international swimmers. I pushed past six to eight sombre, gruff-voiced East German female swimmers locked in a team meeting with an even more sombre coach. They had commandeered four massage tables beside the warm-up pool.

"Don't upset them," I thought, and turned sharp left, through a swinging door onto the competition deck. "Act confidently," I told myself. "Wear the green and gold with pride. Remember what your wife said and don't make a goose of yourself. Better to say nothing and be thought a fool than open your big trap and actually *be* a fool."

The competition pool was breathtaking. I'd seen it only 12 months earlier as a hole in the ground, with hundreds of busy Korean workers swarming over it like ants at a picnic. I couldn't believe the transformation. Today, clear water sparkled. Colourful non-turbulent land ropes stretched the length of the pool to separate duelling countries. Television lights lit the area more brightly than the best Aussie sunny day. Brightly hued backstroke flags stretched across the pool, adding to the spectacle.

The atmosphere was one of expectancy and urgency as coaches from the four nations allotted pool time marched along the deck, barking instructions and calling times to their charges. I looked at the pool timetable: America, Fiji, China and West Germany were assigned the competition pool, while East Germany shared the warm-up pool with Ireland, Hong

Champions Come in all Shapes and Sizes - David Berkoff

Kong and Great Britain.

"There's Moo, the Chinese national coach. I wonder who that Hispanic-looking coach is? He looks mean!" Thoughts flashed through my mind. "Randy!" I yelled, as I spotted an old American sparring partner and mate, Randy Reece, on the pool deck. Reece, one of America's most innovative coaches, nodded briefly, and went right on concentrating on his athletes. As I had none of my own swimmers to worry about yet, I wandered over to exchange pleasantries.

"Any winners this time?" I asked Randy.

"Maybe!" he grunted.

"Who's your best chance?" I asked again.

"Nesty!" he grunted.

"He's not American!"

"No! But he's my swimmer. Now, I'll have no winners at all if you don't piss off and leave me to concentrate on them!"

"OK Randy, hint taken! See you in the dining hall."

I walked on, looking for someone else to annoy, then turned, unable to resist one final, friendly dig.

"Randy!"

"Yes?" he scowled.

"Nesty can't beat Biondi!"

"We'll see. Bloody Aussie!"

"See you tonight!" was my parting remark.

I walked off, soaking up the Olympic atmosphere. The great sprinter Matt Biondi strolled by. The Americans expected him to do a Mark Spitz (winner of seven gold medals at the 1972 Munich Games). Biondi was a magnificent physical specimen, a two metres-tall giant with large hands, large feet, and a beautifully proportioned body with great muscle tone and definition. He had the perfect swimming body. I watched him enter the water and push off; his technique was poetry in motion. He glided through the water effortlessly and I knew it would take a superhuman effort to defeat him. But to beat him was the stuff Olympic dreams are made of.

Just then a slight and skinny kid struggled by, carrying a

homemade canvas bag almost as big as himself. I watched him, fascinated. Physically, he was in complete contrast to Biondi. He was quite small, of a build that wouldn't attract even a second glance from the ladies. "This bloke shouldn't be here," I thought ... then immediately admonished myself for even daring to comment on someone's Olympic aspirations.

Banjo Paterson's poem flashed to mind:

And one was there,
a stripling on a small and weedy beast;
He was something like a racehorse undersized,
With a touch of Timor pony -
three parts thoroughbred at least -
And such as are by mountain horsemen prized.
He was hard and tough and wiry -
just the sort that won't say die -
There was courage in his quick impatient tread;
And he bore the badge of gameness
in his bright and fiery eye,
And the proud and lofty carriage of his head.

But still so slight and weedy,
one would doubt his power to stay,
And the old man said,
"That horse will never do
For a long and tiring gallop -
lad, you'd better stop away,
Those hills are far too rough for such as you."
So he waited, sad and wistful -
only Clancy stood his friend -
"I think we ought to let him come," he said:
"I warrant he'll be with us when he's wanted at the end,
For both his horse and he are mountain bred."

Clancy had faith in *him*, I mused, then turned my attention to the skinny kid. Fascinated, I watched him zip open the large

Champions Come in all Shapes and Sizes - David Berkoff

canvas bag, and shake out a homemade flipper contraption, fashioned in the shape of a whale's tail. It was approximately a metre wide, with a double shoe, big enough for two feet. Once his feet slipped into the shoe, he looked like a merman.

"What's he trying to prove?" I thought. "If he's trying to get attention, he's certainly achieving that - the fool's the only one in the whole Olympic pool with a giant whale's tail on his feet. Bloody idiot!" The intriguing young man slid into the crystal clear water and headed towards the bottom like a sea mammal at play. He moved effortlessly, dolphin-kicking on his back, his side and his front. Like a beautiful whale or dolphin, free in the ocean, he surfaced every ten metres to snatch a quick breath before diving to the bottom once more to emulate the "Man from Atlantis". It was interesting stuff!

DAVID 'FLIPPER' BERKOFF AT THE START OF THE 100 METRES BACKSTROKE

Lawrence of Australia

I watched, fascinated, for 10 minutes before reaching the conclusion that what I was observing was a useless, fruitless exercise for competitive swimming. It might have been OK in the Whitsundays or on the Great Barrier Reef, but at the Olympic Games - no way!

I looked around for someone to talk to. Moo, the Chinese head coach, was the closest: "Hey Moo, have a look at this goose. He thinks he's Flipper," I called.

"Goose? Flipper? Speak slowly please," said Moo, in his broken English. It was then that I felt a hand grip my elbow, and lead me away. It was my old mate Randy Reece.

"Laurie, buddy," he said. "Not so loud. That 'goose' is David Berkoff, the new world record holder for the 100 backstroke."

"That skinny kid!" I asked incredulously.

"Laurie, that skinny kid is the closest thing to a fish I have ever seen," declared Randy. "At our Olympic trials, he did most of the race underwater. He only came up for breath three times. He goes the first forty metres completely submerged. I'll introduce you to him when he's finished."

"Thanks Randy. He uses that big flipper well, doesn't he?" I replied feebly.

Later, I spoke to a remarkable young man with high aspirations: a young man determined to become a pioneer in the sport of backstroke. David Berkoff was a man with vision, one of those rare individuals who prefer to soar with eagles, to be a leader and blaze trails into the unknown - rather than be content to follow the established system of stability and, often, mediocrity.

One week later at the Pool, I watched Berkoff thrill the world with his innovative backstroke style and underwater expertise. I was fascinated by his underwater dolphin duel with Suzuki, Japan's champion. In the final of the 100 metres backstroke, I saw Berkoff slip on his start, and shared his disappointment when Suzuki triumphed.

Later, I rejoiced for him when, as lead swimmer for the

Champions Come in all Shapes and Sizes - David Berkoff

USA, he conquered Suzuki and broke his own world record; then accepted his Olympic gold medal as part of the winning (and world record-breaking) 4 x 100 metres medley relay team.

Life is a continual learning experience for people with open minds. Thanks, David Berkoff for teaching me to never pre-judge any athlete, no matter how unlikely he or she may look. You showed that size is no barrier to success. What counts is the bite in the dog. Dreams do come true if we persist and often the only limits are those of our vision ...

> *And then he ran them single-handed*
> *till their sides were white with foam;*
> *He followed like a bloodhound on their track,*
> *Till they halted, cowed and beaten;*
> *then he turned their heads for home,*
> *And alone and unassisted brought them back.*

Chapter 12

A True Champion
~Debbie Flintoff-King~

At 7 o'clock on a morning 11 weeks before the Auckland Commonwealth Games of 1990, I was relaxing in the lounge room of the neat Melbourne unit of the Flintoff-Kings - Phil and Debbie. Phil King and I were chatting about the values of cross-training and specifically of athletic innovations which might help swimmers, when the front door swung open and Debbie breezed in. She'd been out for her early-morning wake-up jog, and was dressed in a loose-fitting top, fluoro athletic tights and Nike runners.

"Fresh juice anyone?" she called over her shoulder, and gracefully moved into a compact and spotlessly clean kitchen. "Coffee thanks Deb," I called. Noting her frown of disapproval, I quickly changed the order to an extra-large fresh orange juice.

"I feel great, Phil. So-oo fit!" she enthused as she stretched on tiptoes to get a larger glass for my juice. Her calf muscles rippled. Her legs were lean, trim and muscular.

"She looks fit Phil," I said. Phil nodded in agreement.

"We've been to Auckland." "What?" "I wanted to check the track, have Debbie run some bends, check the prevailing winds, accommodation, transport, training tracks, local masseurs and physios."

"Who funded you?" I inquired.

"We did mate, who else?"

"Bit exy, wasn't it?" I asked.

"Doesn't matter, we want gold in Auckland."

"We'll get it!" Deb called happily, but determinedly, from the kitchen.

Facing page: Debbie Flintoff-King at the finishing line, Seoul 1988.

"What a combination," I thought to myself. "A superb team - Phil with his professional future planning ... always paying meticulous attention to detail, and Debbie with her total commitment and discipline. No wonder she's Olympic champion!"

"Where are the Channel Seven studios?" I asked.

"I'll get you a street directory. It's not too far from here," Phil said, heading to the back room. Debbie stretched out like an agile great cat on the lounge room floor to commence her daily ritual - an hour long-plus of stretching and Yoga exercise. I marvelled at her athleticism, dedication, single -mindedness and continual drive for perfection. Memories of her magnificent last-gasp 400 metres hurdles victory in Seoul flooded through my mind. Visions of her desperate lunge at the tape to pass Tatiana Ledovskaia, the Russian, came back with great clarity. This young woman was reinforcing my belief that "attitude is the major key to success."

"Here's the directory - take our car, mate!" Phil's return jerked me back from the recall of Deb's flashing smile at the Seoul Gold medal presentation to the present.

"You sure?" I said.

"Yes, no problem! Deb and I will go in the one car today. We have an appointment with a prospective sponsor of our dream to run the Debbie Flintoff-King Olympic Gold Athletic Camp for juniors."

"Will you get it?" I asked.

"Hope so," he replied. "I'd love to do some talent identification work. There are young country kids out there crying out to be coached, hungry for knowledge of our sport. And there are parents who need educating. Also Deb wants to put something back into the sport that's been so good to her." Phil gulped down the last of his juice and muesli, stood up and headed for the door.

"Oh, before we go. Deb designed a T-shirt for the kids to wear ... I'll show you quickly. See what you think." He rumbled through T-shirts and tracksuits in the clean washing basket, and produced Deb's *Ladder of Achievement*.

"I have to have one," I said.

"Not yet. This is the prototype," said Phil.

"Well, I have to at least get a copy of the words." There and then I sat and wrote them out:

LADDER OF ACHIEVEMENT

100%	*I did.*
90%	*I will.*
80%	*I can.*
70%	*I think I can.*
60%	*I might.*
50%	*I think I might.*
40%	*What is it?*
30%	*I wish I could.*
20%	*I don't know how.*
10%	*I can't.*
0%	*I won't.*

"C'mon, you'll be late! I'll show you how to get out. I can't have you being late for the 'Bert Newton Show'," said Phil.

"No! I'm looking forward to meeting Bert," I said as I grabbed my coat, straightened my tie, glanced in the mirror and ran my fingers quickly through my hair, before giving chase. "Wait for me!" I called.

Phil was already at the lift waiting.

We took the lift to the basement in silence. It has always intrigued me why people don't talk in lifts. I vowed that henceforth I would always talk in lifts. We threaded our way through narrow, concrete passageways to the car park and Phil threw me the keys. "Jump in, reverse out and follow me. I'll show you how to get out," he yelled over his shoulder as he headed for the exit.

I threw my bag into the boot, onto a pile of papers and socks. Firstly, I had to move a large training pace clock, four pairs of Nike spikes and two sets of starting blocks. Typical coach's car, I thought. But at least it was a hell of a lot better organised and the boot was neater than that belonging to the grand old man of Australian swimming, Forbes Carlile. Phil's car was the Hilton compared to Forbes'. They reckoned Forbes' old machine hadn't been tidied since the day he bought it after the 1956 Olympics.

Phil was already at the electronic gate. "Hurry up - reverse it out! I've got more to do than waste time on potential TV personalities. There are Commonwealth gold medals to be won"

"Hold on, I can't work the gears. I'm not bloody Dick Johnson!" I shouted back.

My trouble had started. I was thankful Phil hadn't seen me stall Deb's car three times as I tried to get out without hitting that bloody big concrete post.

"Why do they always place these things near where I have to drive?" I thought.

"That's third gear," Phil shouted. "Put the car in first gear to start." He reached in through the open window and took the magnetic plate from under the dash. "If you put this plate flat onto that electronic gadget over there the gate will open." True to his word, the big steel security gates rumbled open.

"Bit fancy for a Queensland boy! I've never seen that before," I called.

I fumbled to find first gear, and the gate slammed shut! I had a fleeting visions of the huge steel gate crashing down onto the bonnet of Deb's shining new BMW.

"You've got 10 seconds to get out once the gate is up," said Phil, re-assuringly. "Show a bit of courage. Time it right and you'll have no problems."

I started to sweat. "This is a BMW," I thought. "Deb's BMW." Why hadn't I taken a cab? Phil put the magnetic plate onto the electronic gadget once more - and the huge steel gates rumbled up again.

"Go!" he yelled. I stalled the car again. Beads of sweat appeared on my brow. My skin went clammy, my hands

A True Champion - Debbie Flintoff-King

sweaty, my throat dry. My heart started to pump - really pump. More pressure here than at the Olympics, I thought.

Where's Armstrong? Where's the animal? He's good in a pressure situation. The giant gate slammed shut again.

"A bloke got caught under there last week," remarked Phil. "Stuffed his car."

"I'll get a cab, save trouble," I answered.

"Two grand to fix his bonnet."

"I'll get a cab."

"You will not. Debbie won't hear of it!"

"I'll get a cab."

"Don't worry, it's Deb's car."

"I'll get a cab."

"No guts, no glory, boy. Go for it."

"I'll get a cab."

"No way!" He hit the electronic gadget once more and yelled "Go!"

Words I had uttered to my young charges thousands of times flashed into my subconscious: "Never consider failure!" How I escaped that garage is a miracle - but pride is a great motivator, and my pride wouldn't let Mr Phil King - Athletics Coaching Supremo, and a Victorian to boot - take the wheel and put one over a humble Bananabender.

Five minutes later, out on the road, my heart rate returned to something like normal, and I began to loosen up. The radio was blaring and I started to whistle the DJ's morning drive-time selection: *Don't Worry, Be Happy*. Melbourne's morning peak hour on St Kilda road is an experience not to be missed: cars bumper to bumper, horns honking, business men on carphones, blinkers flashing.

Remember your defensive driving, I told myself. Ah! Road works - three lanes into two. I waved to a couple of strapping main road guys leaning nonchalantly on their shovels, watching their mate dig up the road. I winked at a couple of school kids in the back seat of a Corolla and glanced down at the BMW's instrument panel.

Oh no! My skin went clammy, my hands sweaty, my throat dry. My heart started to pump again ... it was happening twice in one day. I couldn't believe it. The Flintoff-Kings must take strange pleasure in having me panic. The petrol gauge of the BMW showed empty!

My mind raced; I had myself running out of petrol, pushing Debbie's car on busy St Kilda Road or, worse still, dumping it and having to hitch-hike to the nearest petrol station. The next five minutes were among the most agonising of my life. As I gently nursed Debbie's car through Melbourne's peak-hour traffic, frantically searching for petrol and being extra-careful not to rev the motor, little cliches with which I regularly assailed my young charges kept flashing through my mind. "By failing to prepare you are preparing to fail". Why hadn't I checked the petrol gauge? Did Phil have a spare tank in the boot? No - only those bloody Nike running spikes!

And then, at last, a station! I flashed the blinker, did a quick U-eee, gave the forks to some guy who abused me and coasted into the petrol station up to the super pump. Phew! A large red-faced man with a slightly greying moustache came from the office, smiling and wiping his hands with an oily rag.

"Fill 'er up mate!" I shouted. "Don't spare the cost!" I tossed him the keys, thoroughly relieved to be at a service station. One minute later he was back at the window giving me the strangest look.

"Anything else mate?"

"No thanks."

"Oil?"

"No thanks!"

"Check the water?"

"No thanks!"

"That will be 28 cents! And mate, if it's any consolation to you, I've been pumping gas here for almost 28 years, and that is the least amount of money ever spent to fill a tank!"

"You're kidding!"

"No! Twenty-eight cents mate," and his eyes lightened. "Say, I know you. You're the swimming coach fellow from Queensland. You're the silly one, aren't you?"

I was mortified.

I gave him 50 cents and told him to keep the change, and to tell no one he'd met me.

I arrived back at the Flintoff-King's after a busy day with the media, completely drained, but ready to relax and laugh with the fun-loving duo - after I'd admonished them for having a BMW with a broken petrol gauge. Home safe, I parked the car on the street. My Dad told me once: "Son, never get bitten by the same dog twice". No way was I going to run the gauntlet back into that bloody car park.

When I walked in, Deb was on the floor where I had left her earlier in the day. Her normal infectious smile had been replaced by a concerned and sombre expression.

Lawrence of Australia

"Deb pulled a hamstring at training tonight," Phil whispered hoarsely.

"What?" I asked, incredulous.

"She's been icing it now for over an hour. She's going to need all the professional help and courage in the world to beat this one and win in Auckland ... God, why now?" he mused ... "it's hard enough beating opponents without having to overcome injury as well."

"I'll do it!" she interrupted. "I've got to be there. I've put in too many hours on the training track to watch these Games on TV." Her voice choked, and tears appeared in her eyes.

Eleven weeks later the tears rolled down *my* face as I

Debbie hits the last hurdle in the Commonwealth Games 400 metres hurdles final in 1990, as England's Sally Gunnell heads on to victory. No-one knew of Debbie's injury problem.

A True Champion - Debbie Flintoff-King

watched Debbie beaten into second place by the blue-eyed English blonde, Sally Gunnell from Essex. Debbie's dream of winning three consecutive Commonwealth Games gold medals was shattered as she faltered at the last hurdle. Gunnell, much of whose training was done on the family farm at Chigwell, sensed Debbie's momentary weakness as she approached the last hurdle. She seized the opportunity, and ran like a wild animal chasing prey. Victory was hers.

To Debbie Flintoff-King, winning is important, vital ... almost the reason for her existence. She was born to win. At the press conference later, I saw a different Debbie - a woman who so clearly showed why she is a champion. There was no mention of the torn hamstring, the hours spent on the physio's table. There was no mention of the pool visits to try to maintain cardiovascular fitness and leg strength; no mention that she was only able to run *one* complete hurdle circuit in eleven weeks. There was no mention of the late nights of therapy, with Phil icing her torn hamstring, and tenderly running the ultrasonic machine over the injured muscle in a desperate race against time.

There were no excuses. Just dignity in defeat.

Debbie, we love you.

Chapter 13

Doing What the Opposition Won't
~Duncan Armstrong~

As a gangling 15-year-old, Duncan Armstrong was a member of the A.C.I. Lawrence Swimming Club when Jon Sieben won the Olympic 200 metres butterfly gold medal at Los Angeles in 1984. Duncan had witnessed first hand the dedication displayed by the 17-year-old Sieben in his ruthless, disciplined, relentless quest for gold. He had also been impressed by the consistency shown by Jono and his bronze medal mate Justin Lemberg. In the 12 months lead-up in preparation for Los Angeles, neither boy missed a training session.

Duncan marvelled at the intensity of effort in their training, and stored it in his memory bank. He noticed Jono doing the little extras that separate the good from the great. He knew from first-hand experience that Jono Sieben had paid the price for his Olympic gold.

When I returned from Los Angeles I called a special team meeting to hand out some souvenirs, and to relate stories of many of the great experiences that you inevitably have as a member of an Australian Olympic team. At the meeting I told the squad that anyone wanting to go to the next Olympics should start right now, today. I encouraged them to set high goals, and told them that if they wanted to be successful in Seoul they would need to duplicate Jono's feat at training - plus add a few little extras of their own. I saw this as a positive

Facing page: Duncan Armstrong with the spoils of victory in Seoul.
At his shoulder, the great American Matt Biondi can only contemplate
what might have been.

motivational move to keep our gold medal factory working. The team did not disappoint me.

The first indication that Duncan Armstrong had the potential to be competitive internationally came in the 1986 Commonwealth Games in Edinburgh. Here Duncan won a gold medal in the 400 metres freestyle, after a magnificent race in which the tearaway Englishman, Kevin Boyd, was almost 25 metres in front of Duncan at the halfway mark. At this stage the Aussie team members had lost all hope of Duncan winning. Many were sitting in the stand only half interested.

Spectators could not believe their eyes - and neither could I - when Duncan made his move. With a wonderful surge he caught and passed Boyd in a finish that had Norman May in raptures.

This is how the veteran broadcaster captured the moment:

"Now, how is it possible to catch a swimmer of this nature, with this little course left?

"One hundred and twenty-five metres to go and the margin is probably six or seven metres. Now, if Armstrong can close that gap, he's a phenomenon. But Armstrong is a man who is pulling right away from the field. Now, coming up to this turn at the 300 mark and look at that - 53 ... it's very, very fast.

"So, round into the final 100 metres. The crowd is getting very, very excited.

"The English team over there on the far side - look at them cheer him on.

"Now, here's Duncan Armstrong coming at him. Just watch this, if Armstrong comes up now.

"Has he gone out too fast? ... this will tell on him in this last 50 metres. He's really flying but Armstrong's coming at him. There's not much there ... look at the margin now.

"This is sensational! I think Armstrong will win this. You won't believe it.

"Look at the Englishman - he's dead tired.

"Armstrong goes round into the final turn. A beautiful turn.

Doing What the Opposition Won't - Duncan Armstrong

"Let's watch this ... down the last lap.

"Duncan Armstrong has got him ... he's ...

"It's absolutely sensational! He was 12 metres behind at one stage and the Australian Duncan Armstrong has gone right past him. What a magnificent ...

"Duncan Armstrong, a perfect performance.

"The Australians are going crazy over on the far side. Have you ever seen a swim like that?

"He's going to beat him ... he's beaten him ... he's given him 25 metres ... 25 metres!

"3:52.25 for Duncan Armstrong - easily his best. It's very close to the Commonwealth record, only a second and a half outside. And what a bold performance to let someone get that far in front!

May described Armstrong's surge as "the fastest finish I've ever seen in the history of swimming."

It was from that gold medal swim in Edinburgh that Duncan not only realised but, more importantly, *believed* he had what it would take to go on to win Olympic gold in Seoul.

Laurie and Duncan, Seoul 1988.

The night of the race, we made a pact. I was standing on the pool deck under the diving tower, wearing my Scottish kilt and tartan cap, when Duncan walked up after the presentation ceremony.

"Show us your medal!" I ordered, thrusting out my hand.

"Congratulations!" I beamed.

"Ta mate! We did it!" he said modestly, and shook my hand firmly. "Dad will like this. He helped me do my wheels at night. He'll be rapt."

Trust Duncan to think of his family at such a time.

We stood side be side under the tower soaking up the atmosphere, overcome by the enormity of the occasion. Duncan was first to break the silence. He turned to me and said simply: "I want to win in Seoul."

"You'll have to do a Jono!" I replied.

"I'll do better mate," he answered. You give me any training you like. I mightn't like it, but I'll do it. Anything. I'll do whatever you think it takes. We're a team."

"Congratulations Dunc!" yelled Suzie Baumer, planting a kiss on his cheek as she headed for the warm-up pool.

Then she was gone.

I looked at him and said simply: "Miss no training for two years. Miss no training until you stand on the pool deck in Seoul! Do everything right to prepare yourself for gold."

He gripped my hand firmly, and the pact was made. Together we now had a specific, clearly identifiable objective.

It was a tremendously tough assignment when you consider that swimmers train *eleven* sessions a week: in the pool six mornings a week from 5am to 7.30am; back to the pool again at 3.30pm. Often during the little time available in the middle of the day, the dedicated few who want to be Olympic champions, who want to stand up on the winner's dais, do the things that other swimmers are not prepared to do. These people with their clearly definable objectives work out further, doing cross-training. They ride, run or spend extra time in the gym, or perform any of the 101 little extra things which give total confidence. When champions stand on the block before the starter's gun goes, they have the competitive edge. They have the confidence to look across the pool at all their rivals and say: "I'm ready, are you?" When that time comes the real winner is able to say: "I could not have done one thing more to prepare better."

The real winner can look at his opponents without fear, and say: "I'm ready to race!" He or she can do this because:

The will to win is the will to prepare to win.

The first 12 months passed uneventfully. Duncan never once missed a training session. I was sick on a number of occasions, and he suffered some injuries along the way, but neither of us missed a single session. A shoulder injury was a problem for a time, and a leg injury necessitated his withdrawal from an Australian team to tour Europe.

At the time he was battling the shoulder injury he would roll up at Chandler with his kick board, and spend hours conditioning his legs and disciplining his mind. When he had the leg injury, he would tie his legs, and float them up with a floating pull-buoy device, and exercise his arms. Sometimes he would come in early and use the isokinetic swimming bench - a machine designed for strengthening swimmers' shoulders. With Duncan, a temporary disability became an opportunity to improve and to condition another part of the body - and he would thrash that machine for hours on end.

I bought two large flags - one a German flag representing the German champion Gross. The other, an American flag, was called Biondi (the US ace, Matt Biondi). I placed them on the floor under the swim bench. The sweat would drip and soak into the flags; perspiration became Duncan's lather of success.

He was determined to do things that would give him the best chance to win gold. Jon Sieben's 1984 commitment was foremost in his mind. He was not only determined to match that effort, but better it. His goal was clearly defined, and because of it he was able to overcome temporary obstacles, and turn negatives into positives.

Lawrence of Australia

Duncan Armstrong, Olympic 200 metres freestyle champion, Seoul 1988. How sweet it was.

The best-laid plans of all of us go astray, sometimes - and what's more 21st birthday parties are fun occasions. Parents, grandparents and young people all love them. A night of balloons popping, people drinking, eating, singing, celebrating, beautiful young women dancing till all hours of the morning. A celebration of adulthood. One night in the second year of our plan Duncan had been to such a party, and had arrived home late.

His alarm rang at the usual 4.30am. It was not welcome and for just this once the dedicated young man turned it off, rolled over and stayed in bed. By 5.30 I had been at the pool for half an hour and had all his team mates working in full swing. They were churning up and down the pool, executing tumble turns, medleys, butterfly, doing perfectly all the little things that would be advantageous to them when they came to race at the Olympic trials in Sydney.

"Where's Duncan?" I asked. He wasn't at the pool - and he

Doing What the Opposition Won't - Duncan Armstrong

should have been. I paced the deck like a caged lion, my anger and frustration bottled up inside. Finally, I could stand it no longer. I turned to assistant coach Ian Findlay, who was my watchdog at such times.

"Go ring him, boy - find out the problem!" I said.

Ian responded like a bull terrier. He loved jobs like that. He was back five minutes later.

"Armstrong has a sore shoulder," he reported

"No excuse!" I spat.

"He said if you can just give him this morning off he will train twice as hard this afternoon. He thinks his shoulder will be right to cope with anything you can give him this afternoon, but he really needs to sleep in this morning, just to give it a rest."

"Bullsh...!" I swore.

Inwardly I seethed. I wasn't buying any of that. Over the years I have coached a lot of swimmers, good and not so good, and can't recall ever coming across one who didn't at some stage need a gentle nudge to get them mobile. A foot in the rear so to speak! Duncan was no exception. I knew he was tired, but I knew he needed to prepare today if he wanted his chance tomorrow.

All of us at some stage, when we feel a little down and a little lazy, look for a short cut. Fact is there *is* no short cut. At times like these we all need a little nudge. I spun around to Ian...

"Watch these swimmers, keep them working hard. I won't be a minute." I turned on my heel, walked briskly out of the pool and bounded up the Chandler stairs two at a time to the phone booth.

"Hello, Duncan," I bubbled.

"Yes Laurie," came the weary reply at the other end.

"How are you mate?"

"I'm good, but my shoulder is just a little bit sore. A slight twinge. I'll be right this afternoon."

"Mate, how are your legs?"

"No problems, they're fine. Why?" he inquired.

"Well I've got a little surprise for you here at the pool. I thought that seeing your shoulder is sore, and that we don't want you to miss any training, you might just run to the pool and I'll give you the surprise."

"Oh," he said. "That would be nice."

"Good, mate - put on your Reeboks then and I'll see you in an hour."

"But ..."

I listened no more and hung up in his ear. I felt better. The 16-kilometre jog to the pool would be a nice little wake-up for him. I went back to the pool deck to coach - cleansed.

Sixteen kilometres and 52 minutes later, a young man drenched in sweat burst into the foyer at Chandler Pool.

"Where's Laurie?" he asked an attendant. "Can I see him? I'm not training today."

It had been a hard run. It was exactly what I was looking for.

I believe that there is always *something* you can do in life to benefit your cause. There's always something positive that can be done to keep moving up that mountain. I figured that if he couldn't swim then he could run, and if he could run then his cardiovascular system would be kept in pretty good shape. And here he was in a lather of perspiration.

He had run hard and was proud of himself, but he was like most young blokes when you give them a tough job - they like to make out that it doesn't hurt. It becomes a matter of "give me any training you like but you won't hurt or crack me". Young bulls out in the paddock butting heads, locking horns, carry on in the same way.

In Duncan swaggered, red-faced and dripping in sweat.

"Well, how are you mate?" I asked.

"I feel great!" he replied, thrusting out his chest and swaggering even more.

"How are your legs? I asked.

"My legs are fantastic," he said. "It was just such an easy run, I can't believe it!"

Doing What the Opposition Won't - Duncan Armstrong

"What about the long hill on Pine Mountain Road?"

"That's not a hill, that's a hump in the road!"

He plonked himself down on a red plastic chair, awaiting a lift home.

"Are they nearly finished?" he asked.

"Yes," I replied.

"Good. I'll get a lift home with Jono."

It's at times like this that I honestly feel I have a slightly nasty streak in my personality.

I slipped over and whispered to Jono Sieben: "Jono, you are not allowed to drive this bloke home."

"Great! Good idea, Laurie! Make him run home. The mongrel should have been here for training. You're a genius!"

"Thanks, mate. Tell the others," I replied.

The joke was on. All the kids were subtly advised that they were not, under any circumstances, to give Duncan a lift home. Nor were they to lend him money for the bus fare.

So there was Duncan, relaxing in the red plastic chair just waiting, reflecting that his shoulder would be right tonight and meanwhile being quite happy to have a dig at all the kids in the pool for having to train. Swimmers are a funny breed; when they are in the pool they work their guts out, but if they get the sniff of an opportunity not to train, then they don't. And what's more, they take great delight in poking fun at those poor unfortunate mates who have been churning up the pool, lap after lap, for two or three hours. Armstrong was no exception. He was delighted to have the chance of a quiet dig at Jono, Jodie Clatworthy, Suzie Baumer, Julie McDonald and Lara Hooiveld, soul mates who also were chasing their own personal goals - to be part of the Australian Olympic team in Seoul.

All of a sudden he remembered the surprise I had mentioned to him. It's human nature that everyone loves a surprise! He jumped up and ran over to me.

"What's my surprise?" he asked.

"Not now, Duncan," I said. "I'm busy. If you can just wait for 10 minutes or quarter of an hour, then I'll sort it out for you."

"I want my surprise now," he pressed.

"I can't give it to you now," I said. "Just sit down and be patient. Wait till the kids are finished and then you'll get your surprise."

He was like a kid waiting to visit Santa and he badgered me for the next 10 minutes. He wandered outside, had a cold drink to cool down and soon was back, asking again, and again. Another drink, another ask. He kept up a constant barrage of annoyance.

"Where's my surprise?"

"Where's my surprise?"

Finally, when all the kids had finished, we sat down in a little circle as we often used to do. At these quiet times I gave out the accolades for training or pointed out mistakes people had made in training. I handed out positive reinforcements that would make the next training session more productive. It's a system I still use. By ironing out little mistakes, and encour-

aging good work, we create a positive environment where all the team search for perfection. You can't hope to be competitive in the international sporting arena if you are not working for perfection on a daily basis.

As soon as we sat down, Duncan wandered over, anxious for his surprise and interrupting the team meeting.

"Where's my surprise? Where's my surprise?"

I looked at him, looked at the kids, raised my eyebrows and said very deliberately and slowly:

"Your surprise, mate? ... (pause) ... NO-ONE here is going to give you a lift home! Furthermore, I can guarantee that the 16-kilometre run home is going to be a lot harder than the 16-kilometre run to the pool!"

Duncan looked stunned.

"What?" he said, in disbelief.

"Mate, you come here as fresh as a daisy. You scoff at my big hill saying it's a little hump in the road. You tell me you're not tired when you arrive. Surely a little 16-kilometre run home isn't going to hurt you?"

"No, he's too weak!" taunted Jono.

"No he's not!" protected Lara.

"Get a cab you weakie!" interjected Suzie.

"Got sore legs, mate?" sympathised Jules.

"Do it, Dunc!" yelled Jodie. "Do it!"

"Run! I'm not going to give you a lift home," said Jono.

"Sorry, I'm not going past your place today," chipped in Suzie.

"See you at 3.30!" I ended the conversation abruptly.

Duncan jumped up and, as he stormed out, looked back over his shoulder and yelled: "I'll see you guys tonight! Now I know who my friends are." Then he pointed his finger at Jono. "Don't ever ask me for a lift home when you're stuck, Jono!"

"Whinge, why don't you, we've been here since five, training," retorted Jono.

"Oh shut up!" Duncan replied, and took off at an incredible pace.

The 16k run home? I was right, it wasn't as easy as the 16k run to the pool - but it was faster! People laugh. The swimmers in the squad did too. He had just run 16 kilometres to the pool and then 16 kilometres home - even faster. Silly wasn't he? So silly that he became Olympic champion.

It is my firm belief that if you want to be successful in life, you've got to do things that other people are not prepared to do.

The difference between good and great
is a little extra effort.

It's a slogan that helps explain why Duncan Armstrong is an Olympic champion, with a gold medal to prove it. A lot of other people, more talented but less dedicated, didn't want to pay the price for the Olympics of 1988. All they took home from

Doing What the Opposition Won't - Duncan Armstrong

Seoul were the memories of Kim Chee and rice.

Duncan Armstrong paid the price.

Duncan Armstrong was the best-prepared swimmer in the 200 metres freestyle final.

Duncan Armstrong's name is etched in Australian sporting history books.

Duncan Armstrong won Australia's 100th Olympic swimming medal.

Surprise! Surprise! I wonder why?

Duncan explains it this way:

> **The difference between good and great**
> **is having a coach who is a bastard.**

Chapter 14

Master Planner
~Phil King~

I regard Debbie Flintoff-King, Duncan Armstrong, Dawn Fraser, Herb Elliott, Murray Rose, Bill Roycroft and their kind as national treasures - not only for what they do for us and for the "psyche" of the country, but also for the dreams and aspirations they bequeath to young Australians - to your children and mine. In them they plant the seed of striving and of conquering, and of making Australia a better place.

The qualities of such champions enable them to perform under pressure in that human zoo of the Olympics - when many others are caught up in the pageantry, the partying, the excitement and the glamour, the discos and the life in a village that never sleeps. Their single-minded focus enables them to perform at optimum level while many of their opponents falter.

An example lies in the marvellous story of Debbie Flintoff-King's quest for Olympic gold which actually started six years earlier - after her gold medal-winning performance in the 400 metres hurdles at the Brisbane Commonwealth Games. This first major win, as a 22-year-old, planted in Debbie the dream of pursuing the greatest sporting prize of all: Olympic gold.

She and her husband Phil started out on a journey, an adventure, that was relentless and uncompromising. It was only after I became friendly with these two great Australians that I became aware of the heartaches and the many sacrifices they made - and how ruthless, persistent and single-minded they were in their pursuit of excellence.

My wife and I were invited to dine at Rumpoles in Brisbane

Facing page: The perfect partnership - Phil and Debbie.

with Debbie and Phil one night not long after the Seoul Olympics.

"Hurry up, Joc (Jocelyn, my wife), we're late for dinner!"

"I'm ready! I'll just say goodbye to the kids."

"Me too!"

We drove into the city, thinking how good it would be to see the fun-loving couple again. I parked the car and we hurried into Rumpoles. No need, we were 10 minutes early.

When Debbie arrived she was wearing a sleeveless dress, just right for the Queensland climate. I couldn't help notice how strong and well-muscled her arms were for a runner. "I wonder how she got them," I mused. "I wish I could get some of my swimmers to get muscle definition in the arms like that."

Half way through the night, with a couple of celebratory vinos under my belt, I could contain my curiosity no longer and burst out: "Debbie, you've got the most magnificent biceps of any woman I've ever seen. How did you get them? I'd love my swimmers to have arms like that." My wife promptly kicked me under the table.

Phil could see Debbie was embarrassed and chipped in: "Ever since the Brisbane Commonwealth Games when our Olympic dream was formed, Debbie decided she would do some things her opponents were not doing - just to get the competitive edge. With this in mind, every day for the last six years, 365 days a year, she did one hundred push-ups, one hundred dips and five hundred sit-ups."

"Every day?" I queried.

"Yes, every day!" she chipped in.

"Even Christmas Day?" I queried again.

"Of course!" she answered. "I reckon on Christmas Day my opponents might rest. That day could be my opportunity to get that little advantage. I'd never forgive myself if I ever got beaten by 1/100th of a second."

(Ironically, she had won her Olympic gold by 1/100th of a second!)

Olympic competition is so fierce, so-cut throat, that if you are going to win, going to be successful, you need an overall plan. This plan has to marry together both the physical and the psychological aspects - the combined factors that help you to train and race. The fact is that in *any* walk of life, if you have no plan you are treading the path of failure.

Phil was the perfect architect. He made plans, and his planning was professional and total - and the execution nothing short of poetic. Physically, Phil prepared Debbie as he had prepared no other athlete. Just as the great Percy Cerutty was a leader, an innovator, a dreamer, a philosopher who used the sandhills of Portsea to prepare Herb Elliot for his 1500 metres victory in Rome, so too Phil King was a modern-day innovator. He was a leader in athletic coaching, a man prepared to blaze his own trail rather than be a mundane follower.

He realised that every job done was a self-portrait of the artist, and he autographed his training regime with perfection.

Phil manufactured a harness for Debbie that was attached to a huge tractor tyre, and three days a week Debbie became a beast of burden. She ran, strained, pulled and dragged that tyre around a grassy oval in central Melbourne, building strength and power into her aching muscles - the strength and power that would take her to Olympic gold.

While many other track coaches were lamenting the fact there were not enough good running surfaces in Melbourne, Phil shunned the traditional training tracks for his own 800-metres hill climb in the Dandenongs. He'd take Debbie out two or three days a week, and she'd run those hills in the tradition of the great Kenyan runners. Eight, 10, 12 times she'd run to the top. Each time he'd drive the car up, and bring her back down. Pretty smart man, Phil King - rat-cunning.

In this way Debbie painstakingly developed the strength, speed, endurance and cardiovascular fitness that would eventually propel her to her historic victory. Phil realised that no man is an island, and he sought expert help, assembling a support group which included a doctor, dietitian, physio, masseur, a yoga instructor and an expert on hurdle technique.

He gathered a team that was every bit as passionate and single-minded as he and Debbie were. They all dreamed of Olympic gold. They were a united team with a common goal.

In Phil's diary the team is listed this way:

PROFESSIONAL TEAM: If required, get specialists to look after different areas if they would do it better than you.

PLAN and INVOLVE them in the programme.

Overall Programme	- Phil King
Conditioning	- Phil King
Competition	- Phil King
Weights	- Phil King
Technique	- Roy Boyd
Massage	- Nick - Sports Medicine Centre
Physiotherapy	- Jack Salter, Geoff Mackay
Stretching	- Steve Barry
Relaxation	- Ian Gawlor
Other	- A.I.S.

Is it any wonder then, when Debbie came round the final bend, applying the physical pressure to her aching body, her mind refused to give in, to relax, to bend? One by one she wore down her opponents. Could anyone honestly believe that with such great team support, with such a positive environment, and having endured all forms of physical pain, she was running for the silver? No way! And so we were able to witness one of the greatest finishes in athletic history as Debbie continued the tradition of Australian Olympic champions.

Having an athlete physically prepared is one thing, but more important still is the psychological preparation - the belief that one *can* win. Without that belief there is no chance of victory. The electronic and print media create superstars, building up an aura that creates, for the stars, a psychological advantage.

Phil set about breaking down this aura that had built around the East Germans, the Russians and the Kenyans. For three months of each year he and Debbie toured Europe on the athletic circuit. They lived out of a suitcase. In Europe, coach

Master Planner - Phil King

Debbie out hill-running, at Moorabbin.

Phil chipped away at the aura by having Debbie constantly race the blue shirts of the East Germans, the red shirts of the Russians, and the black skins of the Kenyans.

The preparation paid handsome dividends and culminated in a silver medal in the World Championships, 12 months before Seoul. Still they weren't satisfied, although Debbie now knew she had a chance. She was now Australia's best-credentialled athlete. The aura around the others was gone. With belief, all things become possible.

In his planning it was important to cover all contingencies, so Phil made a lightning trip to Seoul shortly after the world championships - some 12 months before the Olympics. He wanted to inspect the village, the weather, the track, the food, to search for any little pitfalls that might deny Debbie the gold. He identified food, water and languages as major problems, and set out to find answers. He approached the Australian Olympic Federation about taking fresh water to Seoul. When he packed his bags he included a toaster, Debbie's favourite muesli, a half dozen loaves of Debbie's favourite bread from the local bakery. He took fresh honey from the little farmhouse down the road.

Every morning he was able to prepare and serve Debbie her normal, favourite Aussie breakfast, while this silly b— was in the Olympic dining hall eating Kim Chee and rice.

Phil covered all possible contingencies for the prize at the end of it, for this mighty "team", was the gold that both of them had long dreamed of.

Once in Seoul, his plan of attack was to treat the Olympics as another meet. His motto: *make the most of the Olympics - don't let the Olympics make the most of you.* He wanted Debbie to enjoy the Olympic experience.

He exuded confidence in her form. She had arrived ready to race; the plan was set. He showed confidence in her taper and refused to let her watch other athletes training. He didn't panic when the East Germans were training hard. He single-mindedly stuck to his plan. He was positive when things outside of his control occurred - such as the tragic death of Debbie's sister, and a worrying viral throat infection that Debbie contracted. He reminded her that illness was a warning to the body to rest, and that the gold medal would be a precious memory of her sister. He surrounded her with positive vibes and positive people and never once did she doubt victory. He took her to the swimming, cycling, gymnastics as well as the athletics - and the emotions of nervous, scared competitors, winners and losers alike, were all witnessed. It only made her more determined to give the gold her best shot without fear.

Phil King, I salute you! What a team you were, and are - you and Debbie. Without men of your vision, there would be no national treasures.

Some Memories

Chapter 15

Midnight Madness

Many Australians will remember Wednesday July 24, 1990 as the day we took revenge on "those bloody Kiwis" in the second rugby league Test in Sydney. Only three weeks earlier, 13 proud New Zealanders had humbled the mighty Aussies, led by the Canberra Raiders' man-mountain Mal Meninga. The result stunned Australian rugby league fans, but showed what 13 totally focussed men can do if committed to a superhuman team performance.

The defeat had lain heavy on the hearts of the Australian fans, so the 44-0 public "flogging" of the New Zealanders on 24th July was a very sweet victory indeed. Australian backline star Peter Jackson will remember it as the night he got his marching orders. He was sent from the field for simply pushing a Kiwi in the back. Well yes, he did punch Jarrod McCracken in the face just a little, and he did try to knee him in the crotch just a little. But any red-blooded Aussie will tell you that that's quite OK when you play the Kiwis. Certainly it was no reason for "that bloody Pommy ref" to put "Jacko" out of the game.

Queenslanders will remember July 24 as the day Mark Geyer became an instant Australian hero. The New South Wales State of Origin villain swapped the hated blue jersey for the beloved Australian green and gold and it was just fabulous to see him take out his aggression on those "bloody Kiwis". Of course, the next time he put on the NSW blue again he would once again be: "that bloody Geyer! He shouldn't be allowed to play, the mongrel! Garn Geyer, get back to New South Wales, you bloody mongrel bastard!"

Facing page: Laurie - unpredictable ... innovative.

Lawrence of Australia

Strange thing about Queenslanders - they are single-mindedly parochial when cheering for their own, but fiercely patriotic when Australia's pride is on the line.

Six swimmers training for selection in the Australian Olympic team at Michael Wenden's Palm Beach Pool will best remember that day in July as the one on which looney swimming coach, Laurie Lawrence, announced halfway through afternoon practice: "Next training session starts at quarter to 12 tonight!"

"You're mad. It's the middle of winter," said Olympic gold medallist Duncan Armstrong.

"I don't care! We're going to train at midnight," I replied.

"He's mad!" whispered Hayden Reece, ironman contestant, behind the back of his hand.

"You're getting sillier as you get older! You're nearly 50 now, you know!" laughed Armstrong good naturedly. "You're jokin'!"

"No, I'm not joking. I'm not getting in the water, you are." I then changed to my most authoritative voice.

"We're training tonight. Be ready to dive in at 12!"

"You're joking, aren't you?" persisted Jodie McGibbon.

"This is no joke. Be here well before midnight to stretch," I retorted.

"My dad told me not to come here and train with him, because he's mad!" whispered Jodie.

"Daughters should listen to their dads," joked Armstrong.

"He must have a good reason," reassured Julie McDonald. "I've been with him a long time and he's done some zany, crazy things, but usually he's right. I've never known him to do anything without putting a lot of thought into it first. I wonder what he's got up his sleeve."

Training continued. All swimmers worked hard - each one of them well motivated towards making the Australian Olympic team in April 1992. But you could almost hear the minds ticking over at my strange request. Midnight? Why midnight?

At last, training finished.

Midnight Madness

Training under Laurie was always hard work, but often fun too.
Here (left to right) Julie McDonald, Jenny Burke, Laurie and Jodie
Clatworthy take time out from a Christmas training camp on the Gold
Coast to let off some steam on the beach.

"See you before midnight!" I called as they walked out.
"And bring some warm clothes!" I left the pool, determined to
get to bed early for my midnight madness training session.

"I'll put the video on!" I thought. "I can watch the Test after
training."

I rang the doorbell of my home and was greeted enthusiastically by my three beautiful daughters.

"The Test's on tonight dad" they chorused.

"Let's all watch it dad," suggested Jane. This was the
perfect opening for Emma, the youngest.

"You like football dad! C'mon! We can all watch it. Won't
that be fun?"

I remained silent.

"I'll just turn the TV on early so you can catch a bit of
'Neighbours,'" Emma suggested. She hoped to break the family
rule of no TV for kids from Monday to Thursday while school
was on. Still I remained silent. I knew I was being conned, but
I do love the footy ...

Lawrence of Australia

"Okay," I said finally, "let's watch the Test. Emma wins another round."

"Yeah dad!" they squealed, and swarmed all over me. For a father, there's nothing to compare with the feeling of having his three beautiful daughters jump all over him. My knee collapsed from an old footy injury, and three happy girls giggled and laughed as we rolled around the lounge room floor.

"Dinner's ready! Get up off the floor," called Jocelyn from the kitchen. We ate dinner quickly, and settled down to watch TV and wait for the Test. Emma was deliriously happy. What a bonus! Mid-week TV! The words she had whispered to her mum the previous week kept ringing in her ears: "Don't worry about dad, mum. I can handle him!"

The Aussie team took to the field.

"Dad! Why isn't Wally (Lewis) playing?"

"Don't ask questions. Enjoy the game!"

"I reckon we'll lose without Wally, dad," said Jane.

"Yeah! Wally's the best," said Kate. "We'll lose, dad."

"You girls! Shut up and watch the game."

We won the Test; Emma fell asleep; Mal Meninga, captain courageous, was named man of the match. There was still an hour before training started and certainly no point in going to sleep. I dressed in my old Olympic tracksuit, packed the video tape footage on Jon Sieben and Duncan Armstrong's historic Olympic victories, collected the old tattered Australian flag off the office wall and headed for the pool.

It was chilly outside. Eight degrees. I went straight back inside and put my Olympic blazer over the top of the tracksuit! At 11.30pm on a cold winter's night, a full moon bathed the pool in light. Even though steam rose from the pool's surface, it looked far from inviting for my Olympic hopefuls. One by one the swimmers, suitably attired, filed into the pool in silence. They were greeted by the sight and sound of Jon and Duncan's victories, played on the small portable VCR-TV combination I had placed on block one.

As they assembled, I placed the Australian flag on an old

broomstick and marched into their midst. I had decided to give them a special treat to help them really appreciate the beauties of nature - in particular, the full moon.

"No lights tonight," I called, as the TV blared out Duncan's Seoul victory.

"What?" yawned Armstrong.

"No lights!" I repeated, and waved the Australian flag.

"Why are we here?" asked an exasperated Armstrong, gradually waking up.

"Don't you know?" I asked innocently.

"I wouldn't ask if I knew, would I?" he retorted.

AN AUSTRALIAN WEREWOLF
IN PALM BEACH

Lawrence of Australia

"Well, today ..." I paused, savouring the moment. I looked at my watch to check the time - it was midnight! "Today it is exactly 12 months to go to the Olympic Games in Spain, and we are going to be the first team in the world training for a gold medal."

They stood stunned. "Big Mac" (Julie McDonald) broke the silence.

"Beauty!" she said. "Great! Let's get in. We've got some solid training to do. I need this if I'm going to beat Janet." In spite of having a slight cold, she was first in. Without any fuss, argument or trauma, the rest of my team of highly motivated swimmers stripped, walked shivering to the pool, dived in and trained by the light of the moon. They had two and a half hours in which to crystallise their thoughts. They knew where they were going. The long-range goals were set. They were Barcelona-bound!

I watched them and pondered how many would make it. Could Duncan do the impossible and win again? Would Julie McDonald be my first female Olympic gold medallist? How many of these would have the persistence and determination to keep going? How many would have that indefinable inner strength that separates winners from losers in life and in sports? I knew from past experience that there were going to be many heartaches, many obstacles along the way. These "road blocks" would become a test of the athlete's character. True champions don't just wish. In the tough times they persist and find that inner strength to fight on for their goals. In the long haul, even if their ultimate goal is not realised, many other goals will have been achieved along the way.

I knew there would be stories of both joy and heartache in Barcelona. History would record eventually who the champions were. But I knew too, that on this cold winter's night, under a glowing full moon that we were the first team in the world training for gold as the Olympic countdown moved into its last year. I went into my office and read Theodore Roosevelt's words once more:

Midnight Madness

The credit belongs to the man who is actually in the arena, whose face is marred by dust and sweat and blood; who strives valiantly; who comes short again and again; who knows the great enthusiasms, the great devotions and spends himself in a worthy cause; who at the best knows in the end the triumph of high achievment; and who at the worst, if he fails, at least fails while daring greatly.

It felt good.

Chapter 16

The Gold Medal Bar

If you are a gregarious individual, one of the real joys of international competition lies in the friendships you forge. These may be made on the playing field, the athletic arena or in the swimming pool. They can be between Australian team members, or between Aussies and people from other nations. At Olympic Games, international friendships are most often cemented within the fabric of the village life. The meeting places are many - the dining hall, the flashing discos, the movie theatres, the hairdressers, the games rooms, the coffee shops - or any one of dozens of other little spots where athletes congregate. At these places the world meets, swapping yarns and badges, and talking of training methods, and of future dreams and aspirations.

In faraway countries there are always those exciting places outside the village which seem to attract athletes. In Barcelona it was The Ramblers. In Seoul it was Itawon, a shopping area where you could buy anything from imitation Reeboks to Korean antiques. There you could eat anything from squirming live octopus, to everyone's favourite: a "Big Mac". Day or night, Itawon was alive, seething with international bargain-hunters, athletes and celebrities. The tiny shops were loaded to the ceiling with shopping delights. Inside there was barely enough room to walk and invariably the merchandise spilled out of the doors onto the crowded streets. I used to wonder how they got it all back in at closing time. On the footpath, tiny Koreans pointed and beckoned, enticing passers-by into their shops. The place was truly an adventure land of merchandise.

Facing page: Justin Lemberg ... the trouble started in Edinburgh's Gold Medal Bar.

Lawrence of Australia

The day I visited, Arnold Schwarzenegger was bargain-hunting, stooped over in a tiny shop and surrounded by throngs of admiring little Korean fans. The shop was loaded to the ceiling with leather jackets which, naturally, were too small for Arnie. "We make! We make!" the merchants called, and buzzed like bees around a honey pot.

At the Commonwealth Games in Edinburgh in 1986, the social place to be was a cosy little pub - the "Gold Medal Bar". Boasting a beckoning open fire, the pub was directly opposite the front gate of the Commonwealth Games village. And it was here that athletes from all over the Commonwealth came to celebrate victories, to meet old friends, sing songs, sink a pot or two of Guinness or to simply soak up the Games atmosphere.

It was in the Gold Medal Bar one night that Kiwi swimmer Mike Davidson met Australian Olympic bronze medallist Justin Lemberg, renewing an old friendship. Justin and Mike had been room-mates for 12 months at the University of Alabama and swam there for the US Olympic head coach Don Gambril. Justin, although totally committed, had been unable to reach peak physical condition for the Commonwealth Games trials because of a nagging shoulder injury, and had failed to make the team. His love of the sport saw him arrive in Scotland anyway - as an interested observer and to cheer on his mates.

"Hi Justin!" called the Kiwi.

"G'day mate!" enthused Justin, as he grabbed his old pal's hand and pumped it enthusiastically.

"What ya been up to?"

"Oh, nothin' much. Training for this meet. See you got a day pass for the village," observed Mike.

"Yeah! Let's have a quick pint of Guinness, and go over to the village for lunch!" suggested Justin.

"No worries!" replied Mike.

Just then, one of the wild men of the Australian swimming team, Tasmanian Brett Stocks, spotted the two mates. Stocks waved, and squeezed through the lunchtime crowd towards them.

The Gold Medal Bar

Brett Stocks - sent home and suspended.

"Lemmy, you old bastard! What are you doing here?" he yelled from 20 metres away across the room.

"I'm here to see the Games," Justin cringed, "and to get envious of you guys racing."

"Oh - I'm finished!" called Brett. "It's party time now! C'mon let's get on the piss together!"

"Maybe one or two Stocksie, but not too many," replied Lemberg. Brett spotted Mike Davidson.

"Mike! You old Kiwi bastard! Tell me ..." There was a pregnant pause, then a question: "How do Kiwis find sheep in the long grass?"

"You tell me Stocksie!" replied Mike, although he knew the joke.

"Delightful!" yelled Stocksie at the top of his voice. He elbowed Justin firmly in the ribs, laughing loudly at his own joke.

Two more beers came and went, each sunk in double-quick time.

"I'm hungry," said Lemberg.

"Yeah! Let's go to the village for lunch," said Mike.

"One for the road!" called Stocksie.

"No - after!" replied Lemberg, and the three friends pushed their way through the crowd and headed back to the village.

As the adventurers passed through security, the driver of an official VIP car assigned to one of the smaller nations jumped out and walked briskly inside to talk to a security guard. Perhaps if he hadn't left the driver's door open and the car engine running, the following incident may never have happened. Mike Davidson was first to spy the unattended vehicle. His eyes lit up.

"Let's take it!" he said.

Stocksie, in a show of genuine responsibility, said: "No way! Don't be stupid!"

"C'mon!" said Mike.

"Don't be a d...head!" said Stocksie. "We'll get caught!"

"Ah - you Aussies have got no guts!" said Mike, as he jumped into the driver's seat.

Stung into action by the Kiwi's taunt, Stocksie couldn't refuse the challenge. He jumped into the back seat while Lemberg rode "shotgun" in the front.

"We won't get past security!" said Stocks, as Mike drove confidently up to the front gate. Justin sat in silence.

"Shut up and let me handle this," said Mike, as he eased the car towards the exit.

"We won't get away with this!" said Stocksie. "No way!"

"Relax," said Mike.

"We're bloody d...heads!" Lemberg whispered. "My adrenalin is pumping as though I'm going to race. We'll get caught!"

"Just relax," said Mike and he drove confidently up to the security guard on the gate ...

"Accreditation please?" asked the pleasant Scotsman.

Mike flashed his athlete's accreditation.

"We're due at the athletic stadium in half an hour!" said Mike, smiling.

"Have a nice day," replied the Scot, as he waved them through unchallenged.

A hundred metres down the road Stocksie shouted: "Here,

The Gold Medal Bar

let me drive! Let me behind the wheel!"

"No way!" said Mike. "I'll drive. We'll head to London for the day! It's a great day to see the English countryside."

There must be such a thing as fate, because once they turned into the main street, the traffic slowed to a crawl. Mike put his head out the window and called to a pedestrian.

"What's the hold-up mate?"

"The Queen's in town for the athletic finals. The security's doubled. The traffic's murder!" was the reply.

"Oh no!" groaned Justin. "There's a cop car ahead."

"We can do without the bloody cops," said Stocksie.

"Don't worry," reassured Mike. "They're not after us. They're here to protect the Queen." He held his position in the lane of traffic, and kept driving - as cool as a cucumber.

However, as the three adventurers edged closer and closer, they could sense the police car, containing three London bobbies, was going to block them. "Let's run! Let's run!" screamed Stocksie as the cop car pulled in front of their VIP car, siren blaring. Lemberg, who was wearing a pair of genuine Aussie thongs (made in Taiwan) on the end of a pair of legs (made only for swimming) decided discretion was the better part of valour. "Shut up! Stop - and sit in the gutter!" he said.

The load-hailer on the police car blared: "Pull in here, gentlemen." Once the uniformed police had the three adventurers cornered, the senior sergeant walked over, put his head in the window and asked: "Gentlemen, where are you taking this vehicle?" Lemberg froze.

Mike Davidson responded: "We're swimmers. Members of the New Zealand and Australian swimming teams. We're going to the athletics to watch the running."

"Fair enough," said the senior sarge, "but, gentlemen, do you realise this car is registered as a stolen vehicle?"

"Oh no!" they chorused incredulously. Then Mike, as the senior spokesman, ventured: "We thought it was an accredited car for all nations, and that it was available to take to the athletics!"

"Are you VIPs?" the bobbie questioned.

"No."

"When did you acquire the car?"

"Half an hour ago."

"Where did you acquire the car?"

"Back at the village."

"How did you acquire the car?"

They looked at each other, dumbfounded.

It was right here that the sergeant lost it. He pulled Mike roughly out of the car and shoved him into the back of the police car. Barking orders in rapid succession to Lemberg and Stocks, he pointed to the police car.

"You two, in the back. Now!" Justin and Stocksie obeyed.

He then turned to the young constable. "You drive the stolen vehicle, and follow me!"

The sergeant jumped into the police car and accelerated back to the village. The siren blared, the lights flashed, and the three young swimmers sat quietly in the back like naughty little boys. The policeman grabbed the two-way and radioed ahead. "Car 16 to base. Returning stolen car to village. Have apprehended thieves. Have cell ready, will be back soon. Over!"

Davidson, Lemberg and Stocks were stunned.

A night in a Scottish gaol! "Mate, we're not thieves," said Mike meekly.

"Shut up!" replied the sergeant.

Back at the village, the New Zealand and Australian team managers were summoned to the front gate. The Kiwi manager arrived armed with New Zealand ties and pins, keen to pacify the irate policeman and the Scottish officials. Tom Brazier, the Australian team manager, arrived white-faced and nervous.

"What have you done this time, Stocksie?' he asked.

"Nothin' Mr Brazier," replied Stocks innocently. The two officials disappeared into the office. Half an hour later, the New Zealand manager re-appeared.

"The old tie trick didn't work this time fellas. You are in a bit of trouble," he said. "C'mon Mike!" he called, and jerked

The Gold Medal Bar

his head in the direction of the village. Davidson jumped up. "See ya fellas!" he called, and meekly followed his team manager back to the village.

This left the two Australians alone, sitting staring at each other in stony silence. Each was occupied with his own thoughts. After a further half an hour a drained Australian team manager, Tom Brazier, emerged. He looked at Lemberg and said: "You can go. You're lucky, they are not going to press charges. You're not on the official team, so there's nothing I can do to discipline you." Then he turned to Stocksie and said: "As for you, there'll be a meeting of the team management over this incident. I'll let you know the outcome later." The two Aussies stood up, relieved it was over, and went their separate ways.

Brett Stocks was sent home, and suspended from competitive swimming for two years. Justin Lemberg thanked his lucky stars. Mike Davidson was forgiven.

The message of this story for any sportsman is clear: one thoughtless moment can cost you dearly.

Chapter 17

You Need Friends

After Neil Brooks swam his magnificent anchor leg for Australia's gold medal-winning medley relay team at the Moscow Olympics of 1980, he was inundated with scholarship offers from various universities in the US Brooksie - as the affable West Australian giant is known - finally settled on the University of Arkansas. There he instantly hit it off with the head coach Sam Frieze, a big bear of a man, whose laid-back personality and relaxed coaching style were perfect for Neil.

Brooks was undoubtedly the star of the Arkansas University swim team, and during the college season posted a number of outstanding sprint performances. These not only earned him respect on the American college swim circuit, but also drew the swimmer and his coach closer together. Neil came to thoroughly respect Sam's judgment.

By the time Neil returned to Australia for the Commonwealth Games trials he had total confidence in Sam's coaching knowledge and techniques. He would phone Sam regularly for a chat and for advice. The two had formed a close bond - the kind which helps athletes perform at their very best. The confidence athletes have in their coach is directly manifested in their own confidence, and performance.

The Australian Commonwealth Games swimming trials were completed, and the XII Commonwealth Games team for

Facing page: The mean machine, (left to right, Matthew Renshaw, Greg Fasala, Mark Stockwell, Neil Brooks (in water), pictured here in 1986) became the personality boys of Australian swimming. But the phenomenon of the skinhead swimmers may never have happened if their leader Brooks had not received some official support after a certain incident before the Commonwealth Games of 1982.

Lawrence of Australia

Brisbane, 1982 had just been chosen. The Canadians, Australia's traditional rivals, had decided on an early training camp in Hawaii, and were already in Honolulu - training hard, surfing and exercising, brown, fit and happy in the perfect training environment. They were preparing for the "Battle of Brisbane".

The Australian Swimming Union had to act quickly to make up lost ground. In their "wisdom" they chose Sydney as their training venue, and installed the young Australian swim team in the Coogee Migrant Hostel, with Jeff Hare as the team manager.

This was my first time as a coach on a Commonwealth Games team, so I was something of a new boy. Even so, I was more than a little mystified by the decision to put Australia's elite swimmers in this venue. The accommodation was certainly not five-star! This must be how they toughen up the athletes, I thought.

We had just arrived at our new "home" under weeping Sydney skies. I strolled under the covered walkway, dodging migrant kids on skateboards, wondering if any of them would turn out to have the guts and drive of a Sir Peter Abeles or a Sir Tristan Antico. Both men were migrants who, by guts, desire, determination and persistence were able to succeed and contribute to making this country great.

Howls of laughter from the Australian team quarters jarred my day-dreaming, and caused me to quicken my pace and hurry into the room occupied by Graeme Brewer and Neil Brooks. The two large men lay stretched out on beds which appeared to be designed specifically for Sneezy and Dopey - five-foot beds to accommodate six-and-a-half-feet giants!

"You two look great with your shaved legs hanging out of bed," taunted Tracey Wickham, world record-holder.

"I can't sleep in this Brooksie, I just can't," whined Brewer, shaking his head in despair. He curled up into the foetal position to ensure his feet were at least on the bed.

"Shut up Tracey! I want to swim fast in Brisbane. I don't want to spend the entire meet at the physio's," snapped Brooksie.

You Need Friends

"Well, sleep on the floor you big cream puffs!" responded Wickham.

"It's all right for you, you're a real shortarse. The beds were built for you and the seven dwarfs," laughed Brooksie.

"My body needs a good bed," chipped in Brewer.

"Ring the press then!" exploded Wickham.

She looked around. "We need posters," she said. "These rooms look like the city morgue. We need good rooms. How do they expect us to swim fast if we're not happy? The Canadians are surfing in Hawaii. They are staying in a five-star hotel, eating caviar and living the life of Riley, while we're shoved into this dump eating rice and dodging migrant kids on skateboards. I'll bloody tell 'em I want to win in Brisbane!"

"Good old Tracey," said Greg Fasala. "You can count on the fiery redhead in a crisis."

"Who do we know in the papers?"

THE MEAN MACHINES' BREAKFAST TABLE

THE GAMES NEWSPAPER

Telegraph

FINAL

TOMORROW'S WEATHER: City, Gold and Sunshine Coasts: Light shower. City max. 25, min 13. Bay: Choppy. See P55.

WEDNESDAY, OCTOBER 6, 1982

BRISBANE 52 6011 (Classified 52 0461) 20 Cents*

AUSSIE CAMP TURMOIL

SWIM STARS IN STRIFE

MICHELLE FORD

NEIL BROOKS

ROSEMARY BROWN

By WAYNE SMITH and ROD GALLEGOS

Three Australian swimming stars this afternoon were in strife with the team management.

Gold medallists Neil Brooks and Michelle Ford, with Queensland freestyle Rosemary Brown, were at the centre of the storm.

It was understood Brooks had been involved in a scuffle at the pre-Games training camp in Sydney and the girls, in a separate incident, had broken a camp curfew.

Brooks today would not comment on the incident but lashed out at Australian swimming officials: "It was something I did in Sydney. But they didn't have the guts to take any action over it there and then. They've waited until I've won a couple of gold medals for them.

"I'm being used. One minute I'm their hero and all of a sudden I'm about to be thrown out."

Brooks, a Commonwealth Games gold medallist in the 100m freestyle and 4 x 100m freestyle relay, agreed he could face up to a year's suspension by the Australian Swimming Union.

'Rosemary in tears'

One Australian coach earlier today said it seemed unlikely coaches would seek disciplinary action against the girls. "A scuffle is one thing but simply leaving the camp for a while without permission is another," he said.

But Michelle Ford, last night's 200m butterfly gold medallist, said she, Brooks and Brown had been asked today by swim team officials to sign release forms. Signing the forms would put them out of the team. She said she and Brooks had refused to sign.

Rosemary Brown could not be contacted this afternoon but team members said she was in tears at the Games Village. She is scheduled to swim tonight in the 400m freestyle final.

It is understood the ASU executive at a meeting in Brisbane tomorrow will investigate the incidents.

Relay appeal fails

A swimming jury of appeal today upheld the disqualification of the Australian women's 4 x 100 medley relay team.

The chairman of the jury, Mr Syd Grange, announced the decision this afternoon.

Mr Grange, president of the Australian Olympic Federation, upheld the referee's decision on last night's swim, based on an electronic timing evidence.

Mr Grange said the jury composed of Scottish, English and New Zealand representatives was bound to abide by the rules of FINA — the supreme world ruling body of amateur swimming.

By GLENN MILNE

Mr Grange said FINA rules stated that timing and placings be determined by automatic electronic recording devices.

He said that these devices showed a negative result in last night's swim by the Australian team.

The devices recorded a break of .03 sec. on Australia's Angela Russell who swam the final freestyle leg of the race.

The poolside referee had examined the evidence and made the disqualification.

According to FINA rules video systems could only be used where there was

doubt or failure associated with electronic timing devices, Mr Grange said.

He said in the case of last night's race the jury was satisfied that the electronic devices at Chandler were being maintained and operating properly.

On those grounds the Australian protest had been dismissed.

Australian general team manager, Jim Barry, who attended the news conference with Mr Grange, said the Australian reaction was disappointment.

"But the rules of the sport are there," Mr Barry said, "and we will abide by those rules."

• Girls dejected — Page 3

ANOTHER GOLD FOR LISA: See Back Page

Eye Q P4, Letters P9, Consumer Watch P17, Erica Parker P52, Movies, Services P55, Comics—Crosswords P56, Style P58

You Need Friends

"You can't ring the papers. It's against the rules," cautioned a couple of young swimmers.

"Shut up! Do you want good beds, or do you want to finish up at the physio?" snapped Wickham.

"Do you think we could get good beds Tracey?" asked Brewer.

"Leave it to me," she replied.

And so the 'phone call was made, and the swimmers' plight became public knowledge. It was the sort of story the press love ... and the results of the publicity were nothing short of dramatic. Almost as the papers hit the streets, trucks began arriving with donated beds. All the swimmers helped with the unloading. A now happy young Australian team then spent the afternoon re-arranging rooms, hanging posters and making the drab rooms "home".

After the evening training session, the team manager called a special team meeting to detail curfew times.

"It's getting more like a bloody concentration camp!" snarled Fasala from the back of the room.

"They should give us more credit for wanting to swim fast," hissed Wickham. "I'm going to destroy those Pommie sheilas. I don't need any bloody curfew."

"I'm feelin' caged," said Fasala. "I'm mean when I'm caged!"

"Why do we have to be in bed and lights out at 10?" interjected Wickham. "Can't we be trusted to look after ..."

"Just do it Tracey!" came the rather short, agitated reply from a diligent team manager who was slowly but surely antagonising his athletes by his over-zealous application to duties.

"He's losin' it," said Brooksie.

"He should let it flow, man!" said Fasala.

"I'm going to ring Sam. See what he's got to say," said Brooksie.

"You must have more money than sense!", responded Fasala. "Fancy ringing Arkansas! Save your money - just swim fast!"

"Can't! Sam's good for me! 'Sides, he takes my collect calls all the time. Helps me to relax. I really want to win in Brisbane. I'll do anything!"

That night at 10pm, curfew time, Brooksie, on his fifth attempt, finally made contact with Sam Frieze in Arkansas.

"Hi Sam!"

"Neil! You son of a gun! Another reverse charge call ... you had better swim fast!"

"Sam, I need more speed. I feel sluggish, low in the water. What do you suggest I do this week?"

"Neil you need ..."

"Brooksie! Get to bed - it's past curfew!" interrupted the team manager, who had suddenly appeared on the scene.

"Wait a minute Jeff," said Brooks ...

"No! Now!" shouted the team manager, and he promptly grabbed the phone.

Now this was a major mistake. The only people who could contemplate snatching a telephone off Brooksie would be fearfully brave, foolish, have the IQ of an ant ... or be Mike Tyson. Brooks' normally affable personality changed in an instant that night. In a flash he'd grabbed the manager by the throat and shaken him like a terrier shakes a rat. He pinned Hare against the wall while he continued with his overseas phone call.

"Hi Sam!"

When he had finished his conversation, he politely hung up the phone and released the bemused, terrified team manager. Brooks strode back to his room as if nothing had happened and jumped into bed for a good night's sleep.

"Where you been Neil?" yawned Brewer.

"Ringing Sam," came the weary reply.

Next day, all hell broke loose. Special management-coach meetings were called to discuss disciplinary measures. Rumours were rife. The press could sniff a story, but the team management had closed ranks and nothing was said.

You Need Friends

At the staff meeting Brooksie came within *one vote* of being released from the Commonwealth Games team early.

Brooksie, thank your lucky stars that you had some friends on staff!

Weeks later the villain turned hero. The Mean Machine was born, and Neil Brooks became its unofficial leader. In Brisbane Brooksie collected three gold medals in an awesome display of swimming power, becoming Australia's leading gold medallist at the XII Commonwealth Games.

Chapter 18

Stanley ... Steve Holland

Five am. The sun's early rays filtered through the clouds, gently bathing the training pool at Carina in soft pre-dawn light. The first faint tinges of pink were just illuminating the sky. A beautiful sunrise was unfolding, but a group of bleary-eyed young swimmers couldn't have cared less about that. Each one of them had dragged out of bed at this ungodly hour in a private and determined quest to win Australian representative honours. Their aim was a united one - to make the 1974 Australian Commonwealth Games team to Christchurch.

The swimmers crowded around a thin slip of a boy under the pace clock at the deep end of the pool. They stretched and yawned and talked of the weekend just gone.

"Filthy surf at Currumbin yesterday!" the skinny kid enthused as he adjusted his goggle straps on the back of his head.

"Too bad it was too big for you Stanley!" chipped Norm Rabjohns, National Ironman champion and Currumbin Surf Club captain. Rabjohns was the elder statesman of the group. "It takes a man to go out in the big stuff," said Norm.

"I went out," the youth protested, taking his goggles off and turning indignantly to face Rabjohns.

"Not past waist deep Stanley, not past waist deep," kidded Norm.

"Norm, you know I went out to the shark nets," protested the young swimmer.

"Fair go Stanley! The last time you got that far I had to take

Facing page: There wasn't much of Stephen Holland when he was 15 ... but he broke a world record.

the rubber ducky out to rescue you!" ribbed the Currumbin captain.

"More like the Westpac helicopter!" yelled another swimmer, keen to get in on the chiacking.

I arrived on the scene and barked: "Enough chatter! Ten eight-hundreds. Use the first one as warm-up."

I had barely finished speaking when the youth known affectionately as Stanley dived into the water and started effortlessly down the first of a 200-lap training session. He had two laps on the board before anyone else started.

"It's the only way I know to shut Stanley up, Norm," I said. "Put him in the water. How's he going at the club?"

"Good, Laurie! The boys give him a bit of raggin' but it keeps his feet on the ground. He does his patrols same as everyone else. He's treated as one of the boys."

"No chance of him getting a big head down there, eh?" I asked.

"No way! Fitness-wise it can't hurt him either. He spends about six hours in the water paddling or surfing."

"Good!" I mused, as I watched "Stanley" tumble-turn and slice effortlessly through the water. "I want him to win the 1500 metres gold medal in Christchurch."

I scrutinised his stroke as he sped away, and wondered how I could give this boy the competitive edge. I studied his technique; it was unusual, but rhythmical, strong and correct. It incorporated a powerful two-beat kick that enabled his hyperextended knees and over-flexible ankles to be utilised for maximum propulsion. "I can't improve that," I thought. "He's been well-taught by his father. The only thing I can give him is a philosophy of training so that he will strive to be the best athlete he can possibly be, both physically and mentally. If I can teach him to concentrate on preparing to be tops in strength, mental toughness and physical condition, he can always go into competition confident and prepared to race tough!"

He flipped again, splashing water over my good shoes. It stopped my day-dreaming.

Stanley ... Steve Holland

"C'mon Norm, jump in there behind Stanley. He's six laps up on you already!"

"He sure is! He's like a bloody well-oiled machine. He just doesn't stop or tire," replied Australia's champion ironman, and he dived in on Stanley's feet. The youth looked back over his shoulder, saw Norm and gave a wry smile. With two or three hard kicks he picked up the pace. He wasn't going to have anyone drag on him.

"Stanley" was the affectionate nickname given by the Currumbin clubbies to Australia's only world record-holder at that time - the remarkable Steve Holland. In 1973, at 15, he became (and he still is), the youngest-ever male to break a world record. This slip of a boy with the hyperextended knees, who was always first into the water at training, was destined to change the face of freestyle distance swimming around the world. He became the youngest-ever world champion. He was single-handedly responsible for taking the world record from 16 minutes to 15 minutes. It was Steve who changed all modern thinking on how to swim the event and it had all started on an eventful day at the Valley Pool in 1973 when a young coach with bushy sideburns frantically cheered and waved on his youthful charge ploughing up and down the pool. Steve broke two world records in the one race that day - and thus erased the name of the champion American Mike Burton from the record books.

Two weeks before the 1974 Commonwealth Games in Christchurch, I flew back to my old stamping grounds in Townsville to visit my dad on Magnetic Island. Steve's grit and talent had overcome great hardships and he was now a member of the Australian team in training for the Games. While on Magnetic Island I ran into John Lyons, an old school pal. "Hi mate! I'm off to Christchurch next week to my first Commonwealth Games. We're gunna give those Kiwis a bit of stick! I'm coaching Steve Holland, the world record-holder."

John was a sports freak, and his eyes lit up at the mention of the Games, and of Steve Holland.

"How's he going?" he asked.

"He's just coming good," I answered.

"What do you mean? I thought he was the world record-holder."

"He is, but after the World Championships he hurt his elbow in training for this meet."

"How did he cope?"

"Well it has been bloody tough. He had a needle in his elbow to drain fluid. He couldn't swim for six weeks."

"What?"

"He couldn't swim for six weeks."

"What did you do?"

"He ran, rode a stationary push-bike and kicked for six weeks to keep up his aerobic fitness. He's only been swimming seriously for four weeks."

"Can he win?"

"He's a champion. Champions can do anything!"

"I wish I could go with you!" he enthused.

"What's stopping you?"

"Nothing I suppose," he replied.

"Come on over," I urged.

"I've got no tickets!" he replied.

"Neither have I, but that's not stopping me."

"But you're on the team!"

"No I'm not - I'm just going to walk through with the team."

"You're not!"

"I did it in Belgrade - and the security there was tighter than a fish's bottom."

"You're kidding?"

"Mate, nothin' is going to stop me seeing Steve win! It will be a piece of cake on friendly soil. The guards had automatic machine guns in Yugoslavia! It'll be fun trying to put one over the Kiwis. It'll be easy. It's amazing what guards will do for a few kangaroo pins!"

"I have no money!" he protested weakly.

"Ring Cloaky at CBA Travel. He's always advertising 'fly now, pay later'. C'mon, fly now, pay later!"

"Do you think I could be taken for a swimmer?" inquired John as he started to weaken.

"Not bloody likely!" I laughed.

"A gymnast?"

"No chance!"

"What about an athlete?"

"No!"

"I could be a hammer thrower."

"Yes you could," I laughed.

"What about accommodation?"

"Sleep on the floor at my joint. I've got access to a rugby player's unit. He's away for a month."

After a few beers at the Picnic Bay pub and a few more in dad's kitchen, some reminiscing on the good old days at school and around the Tobruk Pool, memories rekindled of Olympic champions Dawn Fraser, Murray Rose, John Devitt and Jon Henricks, it was settled. John "Hammer" Lyons resolved to be on the plane for Christchurch. Next day, John bought a plane ticket to New Zealand and a shining new hammer - unbelievable! "If I'm going to be a thrower I'd better look the part," he laughed.

A week later we touched down in Christchurch. We were like kids with a new toy. Thanks to the priority stickers I got from a mate in Qantas, our luggage was first on the revolving chute. What luck! We collected it and wheeled the trolley quickly to the exit door for customs clearance.

"Let's get out of here quick. I can't wait to check out our unit" I said.

"OK," replied Hammer. "But first, just let me have one little dig at this Kiwi customs officer."

"Be careful," I said as John sided up to the officer.

"We're here for the Games," said John.

"Good," said the bloke, uninterestedly.

"We should win most of the medals."

"Good," he replied without expression, but the hairs on the back of his neck bristled a little.

"Don't expect the Kiwis will win anything," said Hammer.

"Really?" said the customs officer, quietly fuming.

"We know you won't win anything in the pool because 90 per cent of Kiwis can't swim."

That was the straw that broke the camel's back! "What's in the bag?" snapped the officer.

"Hammers!" replied John flippantly.

"I suppose you train in paddocks?"

"Yep! Sheep paddocks. My dad has a sheep farm. It would be bigger than New Zealand." He was enjoying himself.

"Good!" hissed the customs officer. "Open your bag and show me your shoes."

John looked stunned.

"Your shoes!" the Kiwi snapped. "We have very stringent quarantine laws over here; we can't have any diseases brought into our country via soil on some Aussie sheep farmer's shoes." He turned to me and said: "You're OK, but your friend could be some time." He turned away and yelled over his shoulder, "Charlie, give this smart-arse Aussie sheep farmer guy a brush and show him where the hot water is."

An hour and a half later, Hammer Lyons walked through customs with the cleanest shoes in New Zealand. Round One to the Kiwis! I looked at John. "More bad news," I said. "There's a message for me on the board. It says: 'Laurie, mum needs the unit. I've booked you into the White Heron Motel. You should be comfortable. Jake'."

I collected the luggage and wheeled it out. Hammer Lyons was at it again, this time with a Maori cabbie bailed up. He was giving him an earful and teaching him an Australian haka. We loaded the luggage and jumped into the back of the cab. "White Heron Motel, driver!" called Hammer, and settled back to enjoy the ride and soak up views of the New Zealand country-side. The cabbie sat still, didn't move. A minute later he asked incredulously "White Heron Motel?" For a horrible moment it raced through my mind that we must be booked into some low dive. My fears were unfounded. Fifty metres later he slammed on the brakes, jerked to a stop, jumped out of the cab, stuck his head through the back window and spat "the White Heron -

Stanley ... Steve Holland

Steve Holland at the wall after his record-shattering 1500 metres freestyle swim at the Commonwealth Games in Christchurch in 1974.

one dollar 45 thanks," adding "for your information that's made up of 40 cents flag fall, five cents for the trip, and one dollar for handling the luggage."

"Cheap!" retorted Hammer. "Pay him Laurie!"

I couldn't believe it. What a start! We'd kicked off as a candidates for the Guinness Book of Records - for the shortest taxi ride ever - 50 metres! The cabbie slammed the door, spun his wheels and roared out of the driveway like a young hoon back to the tail-end of the cab rank.

It was going to be a great couple of weeks! We rose early next morning, called a cab and headed for the pool.

I wanted to be there early, a habit I picked up from my old man. I dressed in a borrowed Aussie tracksuit and filled my pockets with kangaroo pins - my pool passes.

I had no formal accreditation for these Games, but I was determined to be poolside when Steve broke the world record. It seemed funny thinking about world records when his preparation had been so badly interrupted by an elbow injury, but Steve was a champion, all class. He could accept the exhilaration of victory and the agony of defeat in his stride. He respected his opponents and worked hard to make sure he could beat them. Even in the adversity of injury, he took a special pride in trying to win and break the world record. One thing was certain - I was going to be there to see him win!

The first thing I had to do was to get to know security before competition started. Hammer dressed in one of Steve's old Australian tracksuit tops that I'd grabbed for him. It was four sizes too small, but it was green and gold, and that was the important thing. We were as ready as we were going to be. I looked at Hammer and shook my head.

"I don't know how we're going to swing it when they see you mate."

"No problems! Remember I'm a hammer thrower," he replied and he tapped the hammer fondly. He'd been carrying that blessed thing since we decided to go to the Games. "We'll tell them I've just come off a course of hormone growth pills," he laughed. "They're Kiwis."

Our cab pulled up outside the athletic stadium; the swim stadium was part of this, the main Games complex. We inspected the track and stood patiently on the pool steps, trying to look inconspicuous as we awaited the arrival of the Australian swimming team.

This was one of the most difficult assignments I'd ever tackled - more difficult even than getting a tired Tracey Wickham out of bed at 4.30 on a cold winter's morning. But once I'd accepted that it was impossible to hide or disguise a 95kg man carrying a hammer and wearing a green and gold tracksuit four sizes too small, the task became easy! "Discipline your thinking Laurie, what is the main objective?" I asked myself. "What are you here for?"

These were simple little exercises that I regularly gave my swim team to keep them focussed and alert and moving toward their goals. The main objective, of course, was to get into the swimming stadium without tickets, accompanied by a large "hammer thrower" who liked nothing better than ribbing Kiwis.

"We've got to get to know security, Hammer," I said.

"OK", how do we do it?"

"Simple! We've got to make them believe we're part of the

Australian team."

"And how do we do that?"

"We've got to watch, be observant and wait for our chance. We must stalk cautiously."

The guards were on a rotation roster, and the new shift was beginning to arrive. We seized our opportunity and smiled at each new arrival.

"Here, have a pin mate!" I ventured to one particularly friendly chap.

"Thanks mate! Any more? I've got three kids at home."

"No problems," called Hammer, jumping to his feet and taking three kangaroo pins out of his tracksuit pocket.

"Boys or girls?" he questioned, as he handed over the pins.

"Three boys!"

"Swimmers?"

"No - rugby players!"

"Really!" exclaimed Hammer, "Laurie here played rugby for Australia in '64 before he became the Australian swimming coach."

"No kidding!" The security guard's eyes lit up.

"Yep! He's coaching Steve Holland, the kid who just broke the world record by 23 seconds." The guard's eyes lit up even brighter and wider. He was really impressed. We had found our man.

"See you inside when the rest of the team arrive," I ventured as he walked away.

"When are they due?"

"Half an hour. We'll wait."

"No! No! Come in now and have a cuppa!"

Two minutes later we were inside, boiling the jug in the security guards' back room, making them cups of tea and handing out kangaroo pins. I felt so proud. We had infiltrated enemy territory. We were in like Flynn.

The swimming team arrived, but by now we didn't need them.

We had organised our own tickets via the magic of kangaroo pins.

A week later we watched Steve Holland break another world record.

Chapter 19

Seoul '88 ~ Reflections on a United Team

The Seoul Olympics of 1988 hold very special memories for me. In my mind's eye still are clear visions of Debbie Flintoff-King's last-ditch dip at the tape for her 400 hurdles gold medal, of Duncan Armstrong's thrilling gold and of Julie McDonald's fighting qualities surfacing as she took bronze behind Janet Evans. But over-riding all, it was the magnificent team feeling in the Australian camp that made the Seoul Games so special.

On reflection, I feel this wonderful team atmosphere was moulded in no small way by Frank Arok and his Socceroos. They helped bind that diverse collection of sportsmen and sportswomen into a true Australian "team". The Socceroos were everywhere. They supported the women's hockey team, and were there when our girls won the gold medal. They crammed into the team bus to go to the basketball stadium, and were there yelling support as both the men's and women's teams went within a whisker of winning medals and collectively gave Australia its highest standing in Olympic basketball history.

In the midst of the many fantastic achievements in Seoul, the Socceroos proved unity is strength.

Hungry swimmers returning from hard training sessions at the Chamsil Pool automatically headed for the food hall. Sure enough, the Socceroos would be there, Akubra hats perched jauntily on their heads, plates of Kim Chee in front of them as they sang *Waltzing Matilda*, *The Road to Gundagai*, *Home Among the Gum Trees* or any one of a dozen good old nostalgic

Facing page: Frank Arok, coach of the Socceroos at the Seoul Games.

Lawrence of Australia

Aussie singalong numbers. The spirit generated by the Socceroos helped crystallise, bring together the Australian team. It gave us a sense of unity - a feeling of belonging. I'm sure all of us felt really proud to be Australians no matter what our ethnic backgrounds.

When the Socceroos slept it was on the top floor of our unit block, and from up there they were always playing pranks on other members of the Aussie team. From this address, a few hours after we arrived, they made and launched paper planes. This became an amusing team pastime until, in an attempt to add a little *more* excitement and colour, they started to light the tails of the planes.

This dangerous pastime was soon banned by the administration, and understandably. The Koreans did not approve at all of burning paper planes being launched from the sleeping quarters of the Australian team. Once this was banned they proceded to throw water bombs on passing athletes. This too was banned. Notwithstanding these minor hiccups, the team would have been a little less united, a little less colourful, without Frank Arok and his Socceroos.

I'm a sports freak, no risk. Once I had that special Olympic I.D. card around my neck, I was like a kid with a new toy. On the way to or from the pool I had to pass the Gymnastics Hall. Every time, I'd flash the I.D. and march in to watch the East German, Russian, Bulgarian and Chinese gymnasts. Their strength and grace was fascinating. I'd sit there among the hundreds of photographers who had come to snap their particular little heroine. Other times I'd sneak over to the cycling to watch our boys - "Charlie's Angels" - or into the weight-lifting arena to watch the grunt and groan pantomime.

As a general sports nut, my shining highlight of the Seoul Olympics took place in the weight-lifting hall, in the achievements of the mighty midget Suleymanoglu, the little now-Turkish-ex-Bulgarian superman. On the first night of competition Suleymanoglu had the "super psyche" applied to him by his former compatriots. Bulgaria's pride had been badly dented

when he sought political asylum after a lifting competition in Australia. The psych-out, however, was dismissed in 30 seconds and Suleymanoglu went on to lift six world records in one night, a feat never before achieved in Olympic weight-lifting history. Australian sporting legend has it that there was an even *better* weight-lifting achievement in Seoul at the Aussie celebration barbeque party on the final night.

Headquarters wanted to give us a surprise on our last night, and they wanted it to be a sensation. The Korean people seem to be able to do anything with their hands, and in particular they have great ice-carving skills. Team coaches had craftsmen carve two giant ice statues: one of a kangaroo and one of an emu - the Aussie Coat of Arms. Each creature stood about six feet tall.

Lawrence of Australia

The entire Aussie team flocked to the barbeque that night. When I arrived, Duncan Armstrong had positioned himself right between the kangaroo and the emu. He clutched a cold tinnie, which he was gently rubbing on the kangaroo's belly. As the night progressed team management were so happy as they smiled and sipped their cold drinks; I don't think they moved more than 10 feet from the carvings all night.

Now, almost nothing can stop an Aussie barbeque once it gets underway - particularly if the Socceroos happen to be in attendance. Our hockey girls, having won the gold medal, were understandably "out of their trees". About halfway through the evening the ice ran out, and the drinks started to get warm. A couple of blokes came over to me and said: "Look, the beer is hot."

Seoul '88 - Reflections on a United Team

At that stage I felt like the Good Lord at the marriage feast of Cana. I popped straight over to our human tank, the gentle but good-natured giant from Melbourne, super-heavyweight 'lifter Charlie Gazarella. All I said to Charlie was: "Charlie, they have no ice."

I've never seen a big man move so fast or deliberately in all my life. He paused for a moment, then strode across and stood in front of the beautifully carved ice statues. He went down on one knee, and joined his hands as he knelt in front of the ice kangaroo: "I'm sorry Skippy, but you are going to have to die for a good cause," said Charlie." Then with a grunt, and with a strange glint in his eye, he raised the huge statue high above his head. He paused for the mandatory three seconds, then smashed the unfortunate inanimate animal to the ground - to the delighted cheers of the entire Australian Olympic team!

The crowd went wild. What a scene it was: singing Socceroos, dancing hockey girls, celebrating Aussies everywhere and abundant cold beer and soft drinks! Duncan wiped a small tear from his eye as he placed his warm can on the remnants of Skippy's tail.

All of it served to consolidate our kindred spirit, and to contribute to the huge success of the celebration party on that last night. It was just sensational to be at those Olympics - and especially to be part of such a fantastic, united Australian team.

Chapter 20

Barcelona Memories

Barcelona '92 has so many memories for me. The smallest trigger can bring them back as they dance through my subconscious. They are not only memories of triumph and victory but of heartaches too, and of the sight and sound of Olympic dreams shattering.

I see Lisa Ondieki's dream disintegrate as she fails to complete the marathon, despite the most gruelling preparation she had ever undertaken. Lisa interspersed training at altitude in Colorado with desert runs to prepare her for the oppressive heat and humidity of Barcelona, but still it went wrong. I picture again the great frustration of the global competitor and world champion Sergei Bubka (born in the Ukraine, trained in Germany and paid by a US company), eliminated from the pole vault as he fails to clear his first three attempts at a height he laughs at in training. Closer to home I live again the heartache, anguish and frustration as my own swimmer Julie McDonald fails. I still wake up at nights crying Why? Why? Why?

But above these are visions of success: of Vitali Scherbo, the Russian gymnast - six gold; of the tiny Chinese elf Lu Li who became airborne on the uneven parallels to score the perfect 10 - a trend started by Nadia Comaneci at Montreal in 1976.

There are wonderful memories of Bangoles becoming a golden pond for Australia - and especially of the incredible "Awesome Foursome". The double scullers, too, Peter Antonie and Stephen Hawkins. The enduring Antonie first represented

Facing page: Peter Antonie (left) and Stephen Hawkins, Gold Medal winners in the double sculls at the Barcelona Olympics.

Lawrence of Australia

Australia in 1977 - when his current Olympic partner was only six years old, just starting school. It was Peter who, after becoming world lightweight single sculls champion in 1987 was told to retire at the top, because he wouldn't be able to cut it in Olympic competition with the big boys, the heavyweights. Like most dreamers Peter Antonie refused to bow to the so-called experts. A fifth in Seoul only fanned the fires that raged within and he pressed on, chasing his golden dream. Fortuitously he enlisted the services of another lightweight, 21-year-old Tassie sculler Stephen Hawkins, who was every bit as single-minded as the "grand old man". They trained their guts out, gave 15kg per man to their opposition - and won gold for Australia against all odds.

Why?

Because they made a personal commitment to excellence - a commitment to themselves to give their all to achieve the goal they set - Olympic gold. Whatever price had to be paid, they were prepared to pay it. So outstanding was their achievement that for me the sight of their exhausted bodies lying in the boat can still bring tears to my eyes.

There are tears of a different emotion as I remember the marathon. The oppressive heat and humidity in Barcelona and that final four-kilometre climb to the top on Montjuic made it undoubtedly the cruellest marathon in Olympic history. It was no surprise that a record 23 competitors failed to complete the course, including the 1988 Olympic champion, the Italian Bordin. Hwang Young-Cho, the winner, was carried out on a stretcher; Koichi Morishita, the silver medallist was wheeled from the stadium in a wheelchair; our own Robert de Castella left the same way. Deek's severely blistered feet oozed blood which soaked his running shoes. In agony he was wheeled to an emergency medical area where Dr Brian Sando, chief medical officer put him on a saline drip for 40 minutes and refused the press access. Dr Sando made the succinct observation: "One gets the feeling that this is not a healthy pursuit when the first three placegetters are carted off in wheelchairs.

Barcelona Memories

We must look at the timing of this event in future so that we don't get the result achieved by the first-ever marathon champion on the plains of Greece - *death*!"

The crowded memories of Barcelona are priceless ...

It begins with 370 Australians from all walks of life called together in Canberra or Frankfurt to receive their precious Australian Olympic team uniforms. They are strangers ... very few of the 370 actually know each other. How do you weld such a group together as a team, I wonder? Slowly over a period of two to three days measurements are taken, people meet in lifts, lobbies, the dining areas - and then there is a team dinner-party in Frankfurt, a chance to mix, and socialise. An Australian rock singer, Juliet Daniels, belts out a medley of rock favourites and finishes with *I still call Australian home*. Members of the Awesome Foursome rise in the dimly-lit room, waving lighted candles in time to this Aussie "anthem". And before you know it the entire Australian team is on its feet, singing and swaying - waving the flickering candles. It is a striking symbol of unification, a welding of people of all walks of life together in a common purpose ... for a common goal, Spanish gold.

For such a night John Coates, the Australian Chef de Mission, has imported two of Australia's living Olympic legends:

• Herb Elliott, a man never beaten over 1500 metres, and whose time on the track in Rome 30 years earlier would have been good enough for Barcelona gold.

• Dawn Fraser, Olympic 100 metres freestyle champion in three successive Games - a feat never likely to be repeated in the pool. Breaker of 39 world records and holder of the 100 metres world record for an unbelievable 14 years. Her world record was two seconds faster than the time Jan Henne swam to win gold in Mexico 1968 when Dawn was under suspension.

These two living legends move around among the young athletes, dispensing positive vibes and encouragement. What a coup to have them there! The night is building now, the spirit of Australia starting to ignite.

Being a bloke who can't resist a good party, and, like all the rest, not wishing the party to end I jump on stage and start the Australian classic: "There was a man from Ironbark ..."

After my recitation, I throw out a challenge: "Can any of you bastards do better?" Equestrian Wayne Roycroft leaps to his feet and screams: "You've left out the last two verses!" I stand mortified.

In the twinkling of an eye the rowing eight are on stage, performing. They are followed by the hockey team and then the Olyroos who enlist the services of the great Dawn Fraser, whom they serenade.

Finally ... happily ... joyously ... 370 Australians from all walks of life are welded together that night as a team. We finish the evening with a rousing *Waltzing Matilda*. Then its

ON TO SPAIN!

ON TO BARCELONA!

ON TO THE OLYMPIC GAMES!

... where dreams were going to be realised and dreams were going to be dashed.

We were on our way.

When you can create this type of team atmosphere, out of the matrix will come your individual champions, your Debbie Flintoff-Kings, your Duncan Armstrongs - plus the others: Kathy Watt, Kieren Perkins, the Awesome Foursome, our equestrian heroes, Matt Ryan, Andrew Hoy, David Green, Gillian Rolton, double scullers Peter Antonie and Stephen Hawkins, and kayak paddler Clint Robinson - national treasures, all of them.

Just re-running their feats on the video brings on the goosebumps for me. These champions give my kids and yours dreams of the future. People like Katherine Ann Watt set up for a whole new generation of Australians something to shoot for - a reason to search, to fight, to strive for excellence at a time when the country is economically on its hands and knees. The achievements of champions can provide an inspiration for

Barcelona Memories

people to work and persist at a job no matter how arduous, menial or boring.

The $64 question is: how do they do it? How do they achieve what they achieve? The answer lies in the word *professionalism*. They have taken charge of their lives; they have worked and planned over long periods. Now, by their achievements, they have become household names.

This is not professionalism in the sense of US basketball's "Dream Team", the members of which collectively earn $140 million a year - these elite of the elite among athletes, who chose to stay in a luxury air-conditioned $1000-a-night hotel in Barcelona, rather than settle in the allocated six-man unit, taking their food at a cafeteria pumping out 50,000 meals a day.

The *professionalism* of Australia's champions is in the way they:

1. Pay meticulous attention to detail.
2. Are prepared to pay the price.
3. Do things their competitors don't.
4. Consistently take the tough option.
5. Are unrelenting in their quest for perfection.
6. Persist.
7. Never compromise workouts.
8. Don't compromise quality.
9. Don't put off things till tomorrow - don't procrastinate. Do it today.
10. Possess that uncanny ability to remain totally focussed when all around are being side tracked.

It is the blend of these winning qualities that enable the champions to keep their cool at an Olympic Games, where parties rage all night, every night; and where many athletes are swept away in the pageantry, the excitement, the glamour ... and the discos. The professionals rise above it all, maintaining their focus and continuing to perform at optimum levels while others around them may falter.

Kieren Perkins not only typified this professional approach, but was able to withstand a tremendous amount of

pressure which intensified as the Olympic competition progressed. Pressure was brought heavily from two sources - firstly the media. As he had broken five world records in the six-month period leading up to the Olympic Games, two of them - the 400 freestyle and 1500 freestyle - at our trials, expectations were high, and the press, both electronic and print, let Perkins, his coach John Carew and the Australian public know they expected gold.

Headlines blared *Kieren our best chance for gold!* Externally he handled the pressure like a seasoned campaigner, but internally the gold was like a hangman's noose. As the competition progressed the pressure intensified ... world record-holder after world record-holder was beaten in stunning Olympic reversals. The great Matt Biondi, Tom Jager, Anita Nall,

Barcelona Memories

What a quinella! Kieren Perkins (left) and Glen Housman after the 1500 metres in Barcelona.

Norbert Rosa, Jeff Rouse, Jenny Thompson - all world record-holders ... all beaten.

Finally Kieren Perkins himself, world record-holder for 400 freestyle, beaten by an unknown Russian, Eugeni Sadovi. Sadovi, who when the Russian tanks invaded his Baltic city took up his bed and resided at the pool to pursue his Olympic dream. The word was out - this was not a good meet for world record holders and the pressure intensified on Kieren.

It wasn't until the last day that he had a chance to release the albatross that hung heavily around his neck. On the final swimming night extra busloads of Aussies arrived at the pool to see Kieren and Glen Housman take on the giant German ace, Jorg Hoffman, the arrogant European who dismissed Glen's out-stretched hand at the World Championships with a simple

Lawrence of Australia

"I am the world champion and you are nothing".

Expectant Aussies crowded into the stands and I started them singing *Walzing Matilda*. They were in good voice and soon little pockets of Aussies scattered through the Olympic swimming stadium joined in. Some waved Australian or boxing kangaroo flags to show their patriotism.

The atmosphere was electric as the announcer heralded the finalists in the mens' 1500 metres freestyle.

"Lane Three ... Glen Clifford Housman." We cheered ourselves hoarse.

"Lane Four ... Kieren John Perkins." Our cheering almost drowned out the announcer.

"Lane Five ... Jorg Hoffman." This announcement was met by stony silence in the Australian camp.

Perkins led from the starter's gun. He was the ringmaster - always in control. He'd worked long hours for many years for this prize and with his goal in reach he would not be denied. His task was difficult, but he realised, as Albert Einstein did, that: "In the middle of difficulty lies opportunity"... and he seized the moment. With 400 metres to go Kieren Perkins got a standing ovation from the world as he relentlessly, remorselessly attacked and demolished his opponents and his own world record.

With Kieren's victory assured I was interested in Glen Housman's performance ... we wanted the Australian quinella. If Glen could beat Hoffman, revenge would be sweet. I raced to the press area, took off my tracksuit and waved it at Glen. He didn't see me, but at least it made me feel good. Glen's victory over Hoffman for the silver was sweet - and Glen was ecstatic. He was not the Olympic champion, but his time would have won all other 1500 metres swims in Olympic history. The competitive spirit that existed between him and Kieren lifted them both to new heights.

Kieren's joy and relief were summed up in his first TV interview, immediately after the race.

"I was expecting both Glen and Jorg to come home very

Barcelona Memories

strong in the last 500 metres. So I knew I had to get out there and get that lead so that I could hold them off. So I'm just so real happy," Kieren told a rapturous audience of millions."

Interviewer: *What sort of feeling was it in the pool as you could hear the crowd outside here screaming and yelling?*

Kieren: "Oh, it was incredible. I could hear the crowd cheering for me. It's just an amazing feeling. I mean, after 500 metres I knew I'd won it once I got two body-lengths ahead. I knew there was no one in the world that could possibly overtake me, and I definitely wouldn't let them anyway."

Chapter 21

Being Professional
~Lisa Curry-Kenny~

The 1992 Australian Olympic team gathered in the foyer of the Holiday Inn, a five-star hotel on the beach front at Coogee in Sydney's eastern suburbs. Kids disappeared from view, sinking down into plush leather lounges, while others dragged suitcases and swimming bags through whisper-quiet revolving doors. In the midst of it Lisa Curry-Kenny relaxed with her husband Grant, the family nanny and her two small children - sipping on freshly squeezed orange juice just across from the piano bar. Meanwhile, Jon Sieben was at hotel reception making *quite* sure that his room had an extensive view across beautiful Coogee Beach.

"I wonder what must be going through their minds?" I mused as I surveyed the busy scene. Jono and Lisa had been gold medallists at the 1982 Commonwealth Games and were the great survivors of the Aussie team.

Jono, heading for his third Olympics, along the way had bagged Commonwealth gold, Olympic gold and a beautiful wife. Lisa had many Commonwealth gold medals, a famous ironman husband and two beautiful daughters, Jaimie Lee (5) and Morgan (18 months). She had long before found fame and fortune - but dreamed still of that elusive Olympic medal. If professionalism counted for anything in her case surely that dream could be realised in Barcelona.

I marvelled at the changes that had occurred over the 10-year period. Lisa had been a star, a swimming sensation at the 1982 Commonwealth Games, a whole decade ago. If it hadn't been for a relay disqualification, she would have needed

Facing page: Lisa Curry-Kenny.

Mayne Nickless to help her cart home an unprecedented *five* gold medals. Now a vivacious, superbly fit mother of two, she was totally focussed again - this time on Barcelona gold! It was to be Lisa's third Olympics as a competitor. She had been to Moscow (1980) and Los Angeles (1984) and had been a member of the media contingent at Seoul (1988). Now she was off to Barcelona.

Success hadn't fallen into Lisa's lap. She explained it this way:

"You make it happen; it may not have happened, but I made *sure* that it did ... you have to be smart, you have to get it and work towards getting it."

"I think the experience, the discipline and the dedication that I've had to my swimming over the years has put me in good stead for now.

"Any little setbacks you have, you learn from ... that's what I like to tell the kids in the clinics and in the camps.

LISA CURRY-KENNY'S WEDDING CAKE

Being Professional - Lisa Curry-Kenny

"There's so much to gain from a sport other than winning - it's all those things that you learn about yourself, being successful and not being successful, that you can apply to your later life.

"And it's the people who use it that become successful.

"I could have sat on my backside and waited for things to come to me, but it doesn't happen like that - you have to go out and find what you want and make it happen.

"Being well-organised is very important.

"I don't have enough hours in the day to do all the things that I'd like to do so I do the things I have to do first ... my days are very much prioritised.

"Obviously there is training early in the morning and I have a good breakfast.

"We've got help to look after the kids, a girl who lives in ... when we are both training there's no way we could do it, so we have help, which is wonderful.

"I put off a lot of business commitments for the last few months so I could concentrate on training.

"We have our own office manager as well; she looks after our business arrangements and basically rings me up at home and says this, this and this needs to be done, or do you want to do this or that?

"But I really like going to the office ... I wish I had more time to sit at my desk and do the things that I have to do, I enjoy it."

The ultimate professional, Lisa throughout her career paid meticulous attention to the tiniest details. Her weight training was unique, designed especially for her. She talked at length to the team nutritionist, Dr Louise Burke, sifting out dietary information, carefully fuelling her finely tuned racing machine with high octane fuel. A sports psychologist, Clark Perry, attached to the team was also thoroughly "sussed out". Lisa's long-time mentor, 82-year-old Joe King, was also on the team, and she would sit for hours with the man affectionately known as "Mr King" pondering sprint programmes, searching for ways to find those elusive hundredths of seconds.

Lawrence of Australia

Hayley Lewis and "Mr King" - the great old coach, Joe King.

Coach Joe King has had a great deal of input into her career, but because he was in Brisbane and Lisa was on the Sunshine Coast, Lisa varied her training depending on how she felt.

She explained: "Mr King might give me a sprint session and I'd dive in and feel absolutely horrible ... so I'd change the session, put the sprints off for another day.

"He (Joe King) is successful because the girls have respect for him and trust him as a coach. We know that he's on the right track. He can be pretty gruff sometimes, not to me usually because I generally do what he says. But he's just a great man ... he's got a lot of good information that over the years he's been able to pass on to the younger kids."

Being Professional - Lisa Curry-Kenny

I had no doubts that Lisa was the most disciplined, focussed athlete I'd witnessed for a long time. Such discipline and drive deserved to be rewarded.

"Lisa, I've put you and Grant and the two girls on the seventh floor in a large suite," called Greg Hodge, the Australian team manager, across the hall, breaking my chain of thought.

It was hard to believe. During my last stay at Coogee before the 1982 Commonwealth Games we were housed two to a (small) room, sharing facilities at Coogee migrant hostel - a one-star place at best! Ten years later, we were in five-star accommodation, being treated like royalty. For the first time, married couples were being catered for as Australian swimming recognised the individual needs of athletes.

Australian swimming had slowly changed to the point where it was now adopting a professional approach to administration of the sport. I mused: when you start treating people professionally you can expect a professional result, and I looked forward eagerly to Barcelona.

Don Talbot the head coach called an immediate team meeting:

"We've got to keep these kids focussed," he said. "Louise, you nail 'em for the diet. Laurie, you tell 'em what to expect in transit, delays, etc. You young coaches - I expect you to look for things to go wrong and head 'em off at the pass."

Members of the coaching staff listened intently for 40 minutes, taking careful notes as Don delegated jobs. I felt secure knowing we had an experienced man in charge - a man who was not frightened to make tough decisions for the good of the team. Team meetings and good communication between head coach, coach and management would be the foundation stone of good swimming performances in Barcelona.

Yes, I decided, Barcelona would be fun!

Chapter 22

Olympic Apologies to Banjo

Don Talbot, head coach of Australian swimming, popped his head in through the door as we coaches settled into the Olympic village in Barcelona in that northern summer of 1992.

"I want a meeting at the pool tomorrow morning after training," he said.

"What for?" I queried.

"We need to plan our strategies for competition. I want a report on each of the swimmers you are responsible for, training times, illnesses etc."

"What about pool times, Don?" queried Joe King who was to be my room-mate in this small unit for the next two weeks.

"I'll know more about that tomorrow," replied Don.

Just then, team manager Terry Buck burst out of the bathroom, a small white towel covering his huge frame.

"Bloody bathroom ... not enough room to swing a cat. When I sit in that bathtub it's like washing down an elephant ... oh ... g'day Don."

Talbot laughed. We all did, as Terry joined in the conversation with no show of modesty. There would be no secrets here.

Talbot left, and we settled in for a good night's rest. Coach Bernie Wakefield and John Carew had a snoring competition. It was no contest. Bernie won easily and next day I helped John move his bed into the lounge room.

After morning practice we had our coaches' meeting at the Olympic pool. It was a fruitful training session. Kieren (Perkins),

Facing page: Kieren Perkins, Laurie Lawrence in Barcelona.

in particular, showed he meant business by commandeering Lane Four ... the lane reserved for fastest qualifiers. From that day on he trained exclusively in Lane Four. He wanted Olympic gold and nothing was going to stop him ... this was part of his psyche.

The meeting went well. Our only worry was Toby Haenan, who was under close observation by the Olympic team doctor for pneumonia ... a cruel blow for a boy who had trained so hard.

"Once competition starts we'll have a team meeting at 7am before we depart for the pool," said Don.

"On opening day only?" asked Michael Bohl.

"No, every day," insisted Talbot. "We have to gee these kids up ... the competition is bloody tough and 26 of them have never been to an Olympics before."

"What do you want us to do?" enquired Bill Nelson.

"Think about how to make the team meetings positive," said Talbot. "If you see a kid over-nervous, out of his depth ... prop him up!" Once racing starts it's easy to lose them."

I put my thinking cap on and decided my team contribution would be a daily poem dedicated to the people racing on that day. So *Olympic Apologies to Banjo* was born ... and read at our 7am team meeting on the first competition day.

OLYMPIC APOLOGIES TO BANJO (I)

There was movement at the village
for the word had passed around,
That the Aussie swimming team was mighty tough.
They had joined the other nations
and felt that they were bound
To kick and fight and sprint and play it tough.

Van Wirdum there with horse-on-leg
was first to mount the block,
She turned and waved to her cheering fans,
she was out to stop the clock.

Olympic Apologies to Banjo

And standing by was Miss O'Neill
just waiting for her race
With half a chance this young girl
was sure to set the pace.

Phil Rogers there, with hair cropped short,
was bound to travel quick.
He looked up to the screaming crowd -
saw Terry wave his stick:
"Go fast young man!" the coach called loud,
"I expect a mighty swim."
"You'll have to swim a minute flat if you expect to win."

Young Shane was there to do his bit,
Joe wants him smooth and fast,
To hold his stroke and kick real strong,
And give the Yanks a blast.

The medley girls were next to rise.
They said: "We'll put 'em to the test,
Those Yankee girls and Chinese chick
"Whose face is not the best."

Hayley, out to prove she's still the best,
will pull and kick and strain,
And by tonight, you bet your boots,
she'll have her favourite lane.

Jacky Mac from way out west
refuses to be beat.
She'll grab her favourite lane as well
and make our dreams complete.

The Two Hundred men are next to fire,
they want to share the fun.
They've come from our fair Southern Land -
there are medals to be won.

Lawrence of Australia

*Kieren's drawn the Italian pair who've
come for Spanish gold,
Little do they realise our boy will make 'em fold.
And Brownie's got young Hudepol, a boy from USA,
But down the final lap our man will hold the kid at bay.*

*So good luck guys. We know you will
Race hard and tough and strong.
You'll do us proud! We'll get our gold
Before we're here too long.
Go get 'em guys!*

After this I threw out a challenge to the swimmers to respond with a poem. Rodney Lawson answered the challenge the very next morning.

That first day's competition was very tough. Hayley Lewis made a final and Philip Rogers snatched a bronze in an exciting race. The build-up to the swimming competition at the Barcelona Olympics of 1992 was in many ways an exercise in unfair pressure - pressure built by unrealistic media expectations. That pressure especially was piled on to the great freestyler Kieren Perkins.

Thirty-three young Australians qualified for the Barcelona Olympic team by swimming times that ranked them in the top 16 in the world. That represented the largest team ever to qualify for an Olympic Games outside Australia. The press immediately latched onto this and began to write the team up as multi-gold medallists. In this exercise the media did their homework very poorly. If the scribes and commentators had taken the trouble to examine the US Olympic trials and then matched trial results against these they would have found the rather staggering fact that only five of our swimmers would have qualified for the US team.

Throw in the Chinese, Germans, Hungarians, other European nations plus our Commonwealth opponents, and it was very apparent that the competition for Olympic medals was going to be mighty tough. The world's a pretty big place, and that's *exactly* what makes Olympic champions so unique and so precious.

The dilemma came when the press asked someone like me: "Are you going to win?"... do you think I'm going to say, "no! we're going to get our arses kicked!" (That would be really positive for the kids!). For sure I couldn't answer: "No! Only five have any chance, the rest are going along for the ride."

The team of '92 was built up unfairly by the electronic and print media in their drive to sell papers and capture ratings. The swimmers traditionally had led Australia's assault on Olympic medals and in that light the media put *high, unrealistic expectations* on the team.

After two days of competition in Barcelona only three people had qualified for finals; the rest had maintained their status quo by ranking in the top 16. By now, the media needed a scapegoat and they went into a public feeding frenzy. They were impatient. They studiously failed to recognise that our best events were at the back end of the programme.

They wanted blood!

By this time the negative feedback reaching the team via telephone calls, electronic and print media was creating extra pressure - representing an added burden that we didn't need during the competition.

"Hi mum."

"What's happening over there? Everyone's swimming so bad!"

The headlines blared: AUSSIE SWIMMERS FAIL!

In fact the majority of the swimmers were swimming up to their best in the morning heats. The need for fast heat swims proved difficult - because we were not used to swimming fast heats. This is something we coaches must address for future international competitions. Future generations of Australian swimmers must learn to swim fast heats to guarantee their places in the finals ... and thus get their chance for medals.

It had been a disastrous day at the pool and the press were

GAMES SPECIAL EDITION

THE DAILY
Telegraph Mirror

SYDNEY, Wednesday, July 29, 1992   WEATHER: Dry, winds easing, 20 degrees   Phone: 288 3000   60 cents*

JUST MAGIC

Proud Hayley lifts Aussies with medal

● Men win hockey ● Awesome foursome time fastest   TOOHEYS

in a frenzy. It was important to maintain the team's enthusiasm because if they lost confidence, performance would suffer. The increasing reports coming back from Australia via relatives and friends resounded with negative vibes and expressions of concern. We certainly had our backs against the wall!

By the third day the team really needed some positive vibes to lift our spirits. I was working overtime to keep the kids geed up; meanwhile the press back home were tearing them down.

We rejoiced at the magnificent results achieved by Kathy Watt and the equestrian team. Those triumphs had the effect of taking some pressure off us at the pool. So it was in this atmosphere that I sat up most of the night and penned a poem for our 7am team meeting. I dwelt on Philip Rogers' success in the breaststroke. I emphasised how proud we were of the whole team, but that we must continue fighting, for hard work and persistence would not go unrewarded.

This is what I wrote:

APOLOGIES TO BANJO (II)

Two days have passed you've made us proud
But the fight has just begun
Relax! Be Cool! Hang tough old mate
There's medals to be won!

Did you see the way our Philip swam
To take Olympic loot
We all cheered him to a man
And coach Terry yelled: "You beaut!"

If you want that gold real bad old mate
Phil's shown us how it's done
Just go and race enjoy yourself
The fight has just begun!

Stand up! Hayley Jane! Julie Maree
Christopher John and Andrew James
You're racing at the Olympic Games

You know our Wallabies beat the All Blacks
So don't give me ifs or buts
Just go down to that bloody pool
And show a bit of guts.

Toby! Nicky! the people home in Victoria
Will go into a state of euphoria
If you two can do your best
And put the others to the test.

Lawrence of Australia

I know you're capable of gold
Don't be left out in the cold
Go out there and do your best
Your Aussie blood will do the rest

And Relay team
You're anchored by a woman thirty
Whose husband's undies I'm told are dirty
Give her a lead or she'll get quite shirty

So let's lift ourselves one and all
You can see our backs are against the wall
We know it can be a disaster
If we don't swim our heats much faster.

You have a choice!
You want an Olympic medal to cherish
Stand up and fight
Or forever perish!

Happy Aussie swimmers in Barcelona - left to right: Chris Fydler, Jon Sieben, Linley Frame and Simon McKillop-Davies.

Olympic Apologies to Banjo

Then we read out a number of the 30,000 faxes received by the Australian team. These faxes showed a fantastic level of support for the swimmers, and undoubtedly helped maintain a positive spirit in difficult times.

Our results on day three were much more positive and productive. Our team was showing great fighting qualities. With these better results I felt the next day's poem should be a little more light-hearted. The team was now looking forward to the daily "Apologies to Banjo".

APOLOGIES TO BANJO (III)

Hayley Jane you've done it again!
You've showed a lot of fight,
But take that bronze from round your neck,
You don't sleep with it at night.

Brownie's old but swimming well.
To-day he's racing Anders.
Just come on strong, use your legs
Pretend he's Summer Sanders.

That's Kieren John, you silly galah!
We know he'll swim his race at last
The way he drives his car -
Real fast!

But Kieren's psyched and ready to go.
We know he's swimming great.
If he can win a gold today
He's bound to crack a date!

Susie! Lisa! How do you feel?
You both look so unreal.
I wish you both the best of luck
Racing that girl with a face like a truck.

Lawrence of Australia

She looks a bit like Terry Buck!
Do your best -
Just show some pluck.

Once again, to-day it's Phil.
We all know he's no dill.
He only dates girls on the pill
But when it comes down to the race
You see the end that's not his face.

A breaststroker gliding down the pool
Swimming faster than a panther
Coach Volkers jumps up to his feet
And yells, "that's my Samantha!"

But Terry Gathercole won't be outdone
He wants his Linley in the fun.
She's fit he says, and ready to race,
She's sure to set a cracking pace.

HAYLEY LEWIS

Olympic Apologies to Banjo

And Joey baby you have seen
how girls can win at just 14
so go out there and have a crack
at winning gold upon your back.

There was a slight pause, and a few laughs. Julie McDonald, my own swimmer who was racing her pet event, the 800 freestyle, piped up, quite indignantly. She thought I'd forgotten her.

"What about me?" she asked.

A good coach must always have the answers. I'd (of course) penned some special words for her and I read them sincerely.

Julie! In you I have the utmost faith.
To me you're like a daughter.
Go out and have some fun my girl
Just skip across the water.

But you must fight babe,
Race it tough.
Be aggressive, cool and bold
And you'll realise your wildest dreams
To snatch Olympic gold!

Julie bowed her head and a few tears rolled down her cheeks. We'd been through ups and down. Today would be the chance to realise her Olympic dream.

Sadly, it was not to be ...

Chapter 23

Galloping Gold

Before Barcelona, Australia had last won equestrian gold way back in 1960 when the grand old man of the equestrian arts, Bill Roycroft, discharged himself from a Rome hospital to ride the show jumps with a broken shoulder to seal a golden victory. What courage, what character Roycroft showed! Bill became a lgened in his own lifetime, in the true tradition of Banjo Paterson's *Man from Snowy River*.

The old man with his hair as white as snow;
But few could ride beside him
when his blood was fairly up
- He would go whatever man or beast could go.

Thirty-two years later at a time when Laurie Morgan, his Rome team-mate, was in hospital, Bill made the trek to Barcelona. His son Wayne was team coach and Wayne's wife Vicki, after her horse broke down, was seconded as an assistant. It became a real family affair. It had been too long since old Bill's Olympic victory and the family hunted another gold medal.

Wayne Roycroft became the architect of that quest for gold. Wayne had ridden for many years, had an Olympic bronze and had carried the flag in the Los Angeles opening ceremony in 1984. He was now burnt out riding, but the fire for gold still raged within, and he had accepted the job as Australian team coach in 1986. For six years he plotted and planned this Olympic assault. Progressively he gathered around him a team of riders that he knew could win gold medals.

Facing page: Gillian Rolton and Peppermint Grove.

Lawrence of Australia

All the tried and noted riders from the stations near and far
Had mustered at the homestead overnight.
For the bushman love hard riding
where the wild bush horses are,
And the stock-horse sniffs the battle with delight.

For me, the most stirring story to emerge from the achievements of our equestrian team in Barcelona was not Matthew Ryan's daring, fabulous gold-medal ride but the ride of an unheralded woman, Gillian Rolton.

Gillian doesn't get a mention in the equestrian team list in the Australian Olympic team handbook. The book records:

Andrew Hoy, 33, farmer, riding Kiwi;
David Green, 32, farmer, riding Duncan II;
Matthew Ryan, 28, farm hand, riding Kibah Tic Toc;
Greg Watson, 26, fitter and turner, riding Tekanga Fred.

Now, I know there was a woman on the team but as I look through the book I can't find her. Why?

The answer is that Gillian Rolton wasn't an original team member. She got her chance only when Greg Watson's horse Tekanga Fred was injured in Europe prior to the Games and he had to withdraw. Then they needed another rider, but the old man said:

"That horse will never do
For a long and tiring gallop -
lad, you'd better stop away,
Those hills are far too rough for such as you
So she waited, sad and wistful -
only Clancy stood her friend -
"I think we ought to let her come," he said:
"I warrant she'll be with us when
she's wanted at the end,
For both her horse and she are mountain bred."

Eventually Wayne called Gillian Rolton.

Galloping Gold

"Gillian we need you and Peppermint Grove! Can you be part of the team?" In the back of the coach's mind was the thought that she was to be only a stop-gap rider. They didn't think they'd need her. Four ride in equestrian teams' events ... but *only three riders score*. The points are dropped on the weakest rider ... and she was rated the weakest rider.

It's history now how fate stepped in during that thrilling event. Our best-performing rider at the time, David Green on Duncan II, came to grief. David had been beautifully prepared, living in England, closer to the high-calibre competitions at Badminton, Windsor and through Europe. However, on that fateful day in Barcelona the best-laid plans of men went astray as Duncan II slipped on a sharp turn on the wet ground, was rendered temporarily lame and couldn't finish the course.

Now it was all up to Gillian. Without her, the woman who wasn't even in the handbook, Australia couldn't win the team gold. The old adage re-emerged: a team is only as strong as its weakest link.

Here I feel a brief description of the three-day event is in order:

FIRST DAY: *Dressage*. Twenty-five compulsory moves as the horses prance and dance a number of tricky manoeuvres.

SECOND DAY: *Cross-country*. An unbelievable day - a day on which horse and rider absorb incredible punishment as they career 27 kilometres and confront from 50 to 100 jumps.

How fit must the horses be? Australia's greatest horse race, the Melbourne Cup, is run over 3,200 metres ... on cross-country day the course is more than eight times as far. It speaks volumes for the training prowess of the coach to get these magnificent beats so superbly fit.

Cross-country day starts with roads and tracks, steady canters and then gallops to warm the horses up. Then ... THE STEEPLECHASE - which is bloody flat-out galloping over fences in which the riders put their lives at risk as they go for it, trying to avoid time penalties. After this come longer roads and tracks. By this time the horse is absolutely stuffed, so they take him into the "10-minute box" for a rest to try to lower body temperature, before they set out on the final ... CROSS-COUN-TRY RIDE.

It's so emotional in that 10-minute box.

It's crowded, horses heaving, horses stamping, snorting, horses lame, riders jubilant - because of great rides, riders shattered - because their horses are lame or because they've accumulated time faults or missed jumps.

Gillian is in here, enjoying herself soaking up the atmosphere. There is no pressure on her. She's part of the team, but effectively as an "extra". Then Wayne walks up, pats Peppermint Grove on the neck and gives her the news:

"Gillian, Duncan II slipped! He's lame ... and David's out. You're it. You're riding for the gold! You're going to have to ride like you've never ridden before.

Ian Greenshields, Chef d'Equipe of the 3-day event, chips in: "We need you! We can't win without you."

The pressure was now firmly on Gillian Rolton's shoulders. She was now an integral part of the team, and it's true in sport as elsewhere that a team is only as strong as its weakest link ... the team needed Gillian.

In that dramatic place at that dramatic moment the course vet walked by. "Oh Jesus," he said. "There's been a bad accident at sixteen. A horse has fallen into an eight-foot ditch; we're going to have to haul him out by the neck and destroy him! There'll be a delay!"

Wayne pushed him aside.

"Get out of here!" he snapped. "We're trying to get this girl ready to compete. Trying to give her positive vibes."

The 10-minute box became a "40-minute box" and Aussie team members gathered around Gillian, giving support. David Green told her how he was murdering the course until his unfortunate slip on wet grass. "This delay is an advantage for you," he said. "Your horse will be far fresher with the extra half hour in the box."

There in that crowded box, the committed Aussies of our

equestrian team began turning negatives into positives; the years of striving, the hard work, the tackling, together, of adversity had welded them into a wonderfully close-knit team.

One of the team psychologists was on hand, ready to work on visualisation skills and positive reinforcements. Nearby, ramrod-straight, stood 77-year-old Bill Roycroft, Akubra firmly in place. It had been more than 30 years since Bill performed his heroic feat in Rome, and his hair was now as white as snow. Old Bill cocked his head on one side, nudged his son in the ribs and asked: "who's 'e?"

"Dad, that's the Olympic team's psychologist. We thought he might be able to help get us mentally ready.

"We didn't need those bastards in my day," growled Bill. "What you've got to show is a bit of guts. Piss 'im off!"

"Fair go, dad!"

This was the atmosphere in which Gillian found herself. Wayne, when he reported to the press later, told them he'd never seen her so controlled, so focussed, so determined. The time ticked away, and eventually it was her turn to ride, her turn to take her life in her hands and to go out there ... for *gold*... She leant over and patted her beloved Peppermint Grove on the neck.

He was hard and tough and wiry -
just the sort that won't say die -
There was courage in his quick impatient tread;
And he bore the badge of gameness in his
bright and fiery eye,
And the proud and lofty carriage of his head

As she left, the old man called: "Go at 'em from the jump, no use to try for fancy riding now."

Wayne's spies dotted around the cross-country course reported back later on how magnificently Gillian rode that day. Her fearless performance put the team in a position to snatch the gold. With the prize before them it was up to Matthew Ryan and Kibah Tic Toc to complete the job.

Olympic history records the achievement of Matthew and his steed. Australian history records how Matthew Ryan, the Man from Hunter Valley:

> ... let the pony have his head,
> And he swung the stockwhip round and gave a cheer,
> And he raced him down the mountain
> like a torrent down its bed
> While the others stood and watched in very fear.
>
> He sent the flint-stones flying but the pony kept his feet,
> He cleared the fallen timber in his stride,
> And the man from Snowy River never shifted in his seat -
> It was grand to see that mountain horseman ride.
> Through the stringybarks and saplings,
> on the rough and broken ground,
> Down the hillside at a racing pace he went;
> And he never drew the bridle till he landed safe and sound
> At the bottom of that terrible descent.

Weary horses, their sides flecked with foam, had completed 27 kilometres and between 75-100 fences by the time they'd finished the cross-country at Barcelona. Their riders were bone-weary ... but how about the horses? They could be best described by Banjo Paterson:

> But his hardy mountain pony he could
> scarcely raise a trot,
> He was blood from hip to shoulder from the spur;
> But his pluck was still undaunted and
> his courage fiery hot,
> For never yet was mountain horse a cur.

So ended Day Two.

Galloping Gold

Equestrian gold for (left to right) Andrew Hoy,
Gillian Rolton and Matthew Ryan.

The horses were ferried home and the team vet arrived. Ian Greenshields, Wayne, Vicky, two stablehands and the vet worked all night on exhausted animals, getting them ready to pass the veterinary inspection next day. They used laser beams, magneto pulse, ultra-sound, modern machinery that alleviates soreness. They even massaged weary horses.

Wayne had the stablehands lead each horse up and down and he and his dad appraised it with the experienced eye of the bushman. They would leave no stone unturned. They picked out sore spots by watching the horse's gait, then they worked on them so that next day the horse could be part of the team. In equestrian, it's not one or the other ... it's a team - man and beast.

Next morning the atmosphere was electric. Finally, the gold came down to Matthew Ryan and Kibah Tic Toc. If Matthew and Kibah could complete the course and knock down not more than *two* rails, Australia would win the team gold, and Matthew would take the individual gold and become Australia's only dual gold medallist.

The team psychologist walked up slowly to Vicki Roycroft, who early that morning had taken Matt through a show jumping dress rehearsal, using Duncan II, who had recovered from a pinched nerve.

"Vicky," he said, "we're going to have to do something positive with Matt, he's talking negatively. He's talking about knocking down two fences."

The old man with his hair as white as snow prickled.

"Piss him off!" He *is* talking positively. At his last two internationals, the horse he is riding knocked down seven rails at Badminton and five rails at an event in Europe. Five rails is the absolute best Kibah Tic Toc has ever done. He's talking real positively. He's talking double gold!

"Piss him off!"

Matthew Ryan now had the opportunity to put all the skill he'd learned over many years to good use. The nine-hour days he'd spent in the saddle leading up to this competition were about to bear fruit. His dedication and persistence would be rewarded. He put on a display of controlled riding rarely seen before in Olympic competition as he nursed, urged and became one with Kibah Tic Toc, riding a perfect round - to the last jump, where they displaced one rail.

It was sensational. Victory was ours!

It's important here that we pause and thank David Green for his great team contribution, even though he was denied Olympic gold by not finishing. How bitter was that pill for a fine sportsman to swallow ...

It's important too that we applaud Andrew Hoy and acclaim Matthew Ryan, but ...

Galloping Gold

... down by Kosciusko where the pine-clad ridges raise
Their torn and rugged battlements on high
Where the air is clear as crystal and
the bright stars fairly blaze
At midnight in the cold and frosty sky.
And where around the overflow the
seedbeds sweep and sway
To the breezes and the rolling plains are wide,
GILLIAN ROLTON you're a household word today,
And stockmen tell the story of your ride.

Gillian, we salute you.

Chapter 24

Born to Win
~Kathy Watt~

My first impressions of Katherine Ann Watt were recorded when I wandered into the Barcelona Games village on that first night in '92, half-lost, dressed in my Olympic team outfit and wearily dragging my suitcase behind. There, outside the Australian team headquarters adjacent to the office of the Chef de Mission, was this vision of a petite blonde, earplugs in, walkman up full blast, crouched over a pushbike mounted on trainer wheels. She was sweating profusely, oblivious to all the activity going on around her.

I sidle up in my smoothest style.

"G'day". No answer.

"G'day". Still no answer.

I touch her on the shoulder, she grunts, spins around and tells me to go forth and multiply ... or words to that effect. I cringe and disappear.

An hour later, job done, she gets off the bike, dripping sweat. Now she's ready to talk, and I'm there.

"What are you doing?" I asked her.

"I'm so angry!" she snapped. They've left our bikes behind! I couldn't miss training so I scrounged these trainer wheels!"

Single-minded, I thought - what a great attitude. Very small, though with strong legs.

Next day Kathy Watt's single mindedness became even more apparent. Her room-mate, Dr Jennifer Saunders, a member of the medical staff at Barcelona, was rostered to start at 7am. This early start was interfering with Kathy's rest and she knew she needed proper rest to race well.

Facing page: Kathy Watt - the racer.

"Can you start later?" she asked the doctor.

"I can't," was the reply. "I'm a junior medical officer. I do as I'm told. I'd like to but I can't!"

"I'll fix it!", declared Kathy and promptly approached chief medical officer Brian Sando for a 9am start for Dr Saunders. The roster was duly changed.

Next day, when Dr Saunders was up early again in line with her habit as an early riser, Kathy promptly asked her to sleep in the kitchen for the next week until her races were over!

Four days later, this single-minded young woman would emerge from comparative obscurity to become Australia's first, ever female Olympic cycling champion and Dr Jennifer Mary Saunders would be there to share the magic moment.

Winners such as Kathy Watt know things of value are not won by luck, they are won by pain, sacrifice, and persistence ... 99 per cent of the time.

How had it happened for this slim girl, daughter of a man who was a marathon runner, a dreamer, a disciple of the great Percy Cerutty? Cerutty, that extraordinary man with vision, who believed in being a leader not a follower; who believed in cutting trails; who believed in going where no one else was prepared to go.

Kathy's dad, Geoffrey Watt, an adventurer, raced marathons all round the world. In his own writings of his travels, *Eat Oats and Fly,* he records how when in Africa he visited the great marathoner Abebe Bikila. While in Africa he decided to climb the country's highest mountain - Mt Kilimanjaro, 19,340 feet. Here's how he records the task:

Alone and without equipment I climbed to the top. I had sold my boots for a pint of beer in Ethiopia and thus climbed in a pair of sandshoes. One day I climbed from 9000 to 15,000 feet, 21 miles' walking in six hours - the pace being forced in the last hour because I was caught in a snowstorm and daren't stop, lest I freeze. The next day I made the peak after climbing for hours in loose snow. At such an altitude I had to summon all the strength and stamina I had before taking 20 steps. Then

Born to Win - Kathy Watt

I would rest and try to take 20 more; overnight I became snow-blind and spent two dreadful days stumbling down the slopes to safety. This experience had a profound effect on me and for a while I was quite fearless and would go walking in the jungle at night, unafraid of man or beast.

When Kathy was five years old her dad went up into the mountains near where they were living in Victoria to explore a new marathon path. A Melbourne newspaper recorded what happened:

Melbourne, Monday September 8: *Australian marathon runner, Geoffrey Watt, 36, was found dead, partly covered by snow on Mount Erica, 135 miles south east of Melbourne, this morning. He was found lying on his back in 12 inches of snow at the summit of the 5000-foot mountain. He was wearing only silk running shorts and a singlet. An autopsy will be held tomorrow. Mr Watt's widow, Kathleen, is pregnant. She has three daughters, aged four, three and two.*

Kathy was the eldest daughter ... from that day she began to build a dream - to achieve something that her father was unable to do. Her mother supported her 100 per cent.

Lawrence of Australia

Kathy started as an 800 metres runner, then became a 3000 metres runner. By the time she was 21 the best she had ever done in spite of all her dreaming, in spite of all her driving ambition, was to place second in the NSW cross-country championships, and run a place in a junior 3000 metres championship.

The dream was still there, though. It still burned strongly in her. Scorning rest, she trained hard - with disastrous results: torn Achilles tendons. She believed as Percy Cerutty had done: *Rest is for the dead.*

Determined not to miss training, she bought a push bike. One day the old bloke at the local bike shop invited her down to race the next weekend.

"How far?" she asked.

"Only 40 kilometres," he replied.

The farthest she had ridden in training before was 12 kilometres, but she went down, and completed the race. Slowly in the weeks ahead she caught the "bike bug" and began to train.

Within six months Kathy was national champion; she knew now that her future was with bikes. She had the flexibility to change course - but to still keep chasing her golden dream.

To make herself a winner, she trained as no other woman had; she decided to train with the men. They became her benchmark. Once a week she raced the men in an hour-long criterium at the local cycling club: round the track for an hour trying to drop your opposition before that last desperate sprint to the finish. In a 12-month period, she won four of these races against the men.

In addition there were five male bike riders with whom she'd ride the Dandenong Hills once a week- the unforgiving Dandenongs that had played their part in producing Debbie Flintoff-King's gold medal on the track. The bunch would ride 160-200 kilometres; five long, tedious hours in the saddle.

And people laughed at her: "You're kidding! You don't

have to do *that* to be a champion."

Finally, on Judgement Day, the Australian Cycling Federation selected four girls to train and race overseas - under the guillotine promise that only *three* of the four would be going to Barcelona. Talk about keeping the pressure on! But it was fair game - you have to have the ability to absorb pressure if you want to perform to your best.

When the edict came through: "Girls, one of you will not be going to Barcelona", Kathy vowed she would not be the one to miss out ... what a lonely homecoming that would be ... no standing ovations, only your parents to meet you ... if you were lucky enough to have them. In France she rode below her best on a new frame she had been instructed to use. The quartet went from Europe to the Americas to compete, the guillotine still hanging threateningly over their heads.

One of you will be going home.

In America Kathy visited a bike shop and bought the equipment her Australian team would not give her. She set up the bike how she wanted it, changed the seat, goose-neck and cranks so she could get her feet in position to get maximum power. Now things started to change. She was third in the Tour of Colorado, an event boasting a collection of class international European riders as well as the US team. She then won the Tallyride stage race - took the overall tour - including the first day, which involved a 21-kilometre gruelling hill climb. Katherine Ann Watt was being noticed. She was flexing her muscles.

The team coach was putting pressure on her to ride only the road race and to relinquish her position on the track to a girl he had coached back home. But Kathy refused to bow. She wanted her dues, and subsequently the coach resigned.

I asked her how she felt then and she answered: "I'm persistent, I'm determined. Nothing was going to stop me from going to the Olympic Games."

I probed further: "When did you decide that you wanted to win the gold medal?"

She replied: "I've always wanted to win ... always, but nine months before the Olympics when I raced in Barcelona at the pre-Olympic trial over the distance, my fifth place made me realise I was close. I talked to my boyfriend, a professional cyclist in Melbourne, and he encouraged me; he had faith in me. He said to me:

'You're only half pace! You've got the talent but you've never dedicated yourself. You want the Olympic gold, you have to do extra. Do what your father did for Percy.'"

So the extra dedication was instilled. She put a hold on her physiotherapy studies, she scrutinised her diet carefully, she changed coach Charlie Walsh's training program ... to make it harder. She didn't march in the Games opening ceremony; she

Born to Win - Kathy Watt

*Kathy Watt, photographed by Barrie Ward,
on the night of her Gold Medal triumph in Barcelona.*

rode 700 kilometres per week; she refused to miss training. With this background behind her she had the courage to attack the field in the Olympic road race with 16 kilometres remaining, to go out alone.

The Kathy Watt story brings tears to my eyes, and Vince Lombardi's words ring so true:

The harder you work, the harder it is to surrender.

Laurie Lawrence

By Peter Fenton

We've had some wondrous people
In the history of our sport,
While some have played at football,
Some have run or swum or fought.

And some have played at cricket
And have driven racing cars,
While some were lofting sand irons
Others lifted weights on bars.

They've come from every walk of life
From every port of call,
The one who stands before us
Is quite different to them all.

He played top level rugby
And the Green and Gold he wore,
The back up half to Catchpole
On the tour of sixty four.

And when he'd done with rugby
He'd not lie still for quids,
He turned his hand to swimming
And to coaching Aussie kids.

The stories of his coaching
We each may well recall,
And those he's helped to stardom
Have thrilled us one and all

We cheered for Duncan Armstrong
And we cheered for Sieben too,
And wondered if our Laurie
Risked a heart attack or two.

His heart is with his proteges
The pain shows on his face,
He's straining every sinew
As his charges swim their race.

And when the race is over
He'll jump and lunge about,
Some staid and bored officials
Just can't work our Laurie out.

If you should stop to wonder
What drives him on, well then
God gave him all the energy
He'd really meant for ten.

They measured him at five foot eight
They used a tape and all,
No matter how they measured him
The man is ten feet tall.

You just can't think of Laurie
Ever growing slightly old,
Lift a glass to Laurie Lawrence
Who is from a different mould.

BECOMING
A WINNER WITH
LAURIE LAWRENCE

Laurie Lawrence is in strong demand as an inspiring and entertaining corporate speaker. His messages of success from the sporting world translate brilliantly to the world of business. Witty and uplifting, he has become one of the most sought-after motivational speakers in Australia.

For further information,
contact Jennifer on (07) 341 7260 (phone & fax)
or write to: Laurie Lawrence
284 Millers Road, Eight Mile Plains, Queensland 4113.

Now available on audio cassette
(at $29.95 per cassette)
is Laurie Lawrence's outstanding
"Gold Medal Collection"
• **12 Midnight**
• **Los Angeles and Seoul Recollections (live)**
• **Barcelona Recollections (live)**

Plus ...
through his strong commitment to
reducing the number of toddler deaths
by drowning, Laurie has produced:
• **A video - "Babies Can Swim" ($29.95)**
• **A book - "Sink or Swim" ($13.95)**

To order any item from the Laurie Lawrence Collection,
phone or fax Jennifer on (07) 341 7260.